THEORY AND PRACTICE OF MANAGEMENT

THEORY AND PRACTICE OF MANAGEMENT

TARA CHAND

MOHIT PUBLICATIONS
NEW DELHI-110 002

Published : 2025 (Revised Edition)

ISBN 81-7445-110-2

Published by
MOHIT PUBLICATIONS
4675/21, Ansari Road, Darya Gang
New Delhi-110 002
Ph.: 3255141, 3284136

Printed in India

Published by P.K.Goel for Mohit Publications, Laser Typesetting by Vinayak Computers, Shahdara, Delhi-110032, Ph.: 2286717 and Printed at ARORA OFFSET PRESS, Laxmi Nagar, Delhi-110092

Preface

Management is both a science and an art. The management of time, personnel, finance, administration, inventory and even market are vital for every business concern and enterpreneur. Managers have their own charm and glamour around their jobs. India is nowadays witnessing a revolution in youths' ideals. A few years back young Indians wanted to become engineers, doctors, accountants, IAS-IPS officers, and even the defence officers. Now every second young Indian wants to enter the corporate world. This book is written with a great foresight towards the art of management. The students, managers and corporate officials will find the book useful for them.

Editor

Contents

Preface v

1. Issues and Hypotheses in Management 1
2. Goals of Management 24
3. Strategies for Success 31
4. Professional Career Development 68
5. Accounting and the Pursuit of Efficiency 83
6. Organisational Culture 113
7. Executive Development 133
8. Prescriptions for Success 150
9. The Commitment in Management 160
10. The Practice of Decision Making 165
11. Reward Systems and Company Culture 173
12. Teaching Management 186

Index 205

1

Issues and Hypotheses in Management

Attempts to improve coordination are only one manifestation of the long historical search for greater rationality in public affairs, but they have been central to the history of social policy. From the Charity Organisation Society and the Royal Commission on the Poor Laws to the Central Policy Review Staff and JASP, the leitmotif of coordination has traced a path through a century of concern about social problems. Motivations and objectives have varied greatly, but underlying them has been a constant reality: social issues, needs and problems—and the responses which they invoke—are usually complex and interrelated. As a consequence, a call for greater coordination flows almost ineluctably from any discovery of duplication, inefficiency, ineffectiveness, or of 'holes in the safety net'.

Perhaps surprisingly, given the historical background, coordination in social policy tends to be regarded as neutral and innocuous at worst and as self-evidently good for consumers and clients at best. We do not make this assumption. Coordination can be pressed to the service of many causes and interests; who gains and who loses from coordinative successes and failures must be investigated, not taken for granted. As Pressman and Wildavsky note, in the absence of consensus and common purpose 'coordination becomes another term for coercion'. More specifically, Glennerster has argued that in recent times centrally coordinated social planning has been at least as much about the control and rationing of public expenditure as about the effective meeting of social need. Similarly, social service professionals who ostensibly seek to improve coordination in order to benefit their clients can easily be seduced by that which is personally rewarding or professionally appealing; they can lose sight of how the consumers actually experience services and of what for them amounts to accessible and useful forms of help. These are matters of evaluation which we did not broach systematically in our empirical research. Our sights were firmly set on policy and administrative processes, not on outcomes as such. Nonetheless, there can be no doubt that the search for rationality which characterised the 1970s was strongly motivated, at least in part, by a desire to produce policies and outcomes which would be better for the immediate client or consumer. We therefore set off in search of coordination in the belief that it—and the wider demand for rationality in social policy which it represents—could certainly, in principle, be in the interests of the public in contact with the social services.

Coordination: Its Meaning and Political Relevance

Precision about the meaning of coordination is rare. We have broadly characterised it as a pursuit of coherence, consistency, comprehensiveness and of harmonious or compatible outcomes. In the 1960s and 1970s, however, it took on a more specific, dominant form. Within the belief in rational, synoptic planning was to be found a search for *policy* coordination—coordination at the strategic level. Coordination was central, not peripheral to the style of governance. Indeed, the preoccupation with administrative technique and organisational machinery was at times so strong that it became the major form of substantive policy. The reorganisation of the personal social services, the health service, and local government could all be seen in this light; so, too, could the partnership policies and 'total approach' towards the inner cities.

Coordination is above all the rationalist's technique for embracing the complexity and interrelatedness of social issues and problems, and there can be no doubt that at times rational planning has come to resemble the triumph of administrative technique over the craft of politics. Planning in the 1960s and 1970s was primarily conceived, by default as much as by design, as a centralised and essentially technical process. As such it threatened to bypass the political masters it was supposedly serving, but it also seemed poised to supplant the more obscure and mundane craft of bureaucratic politics—the bargaining, tradeoffs and fancy footwork by which professionals and administrators in the public services defend or promote sectional goals and interests.

It is important to note and hold on to both these notions of politics: what might be called 'high politics' and 'low politics'. The search for rationality in public affairs usually expresses an impatience, even distaste, for the former and always for the latter. It represents an attempt to marshal and discipline the chaos which can arise from a multiplicity of competing, often conflicting, interests. The political craft, on the other hand, is embedded in the recognition of divergent interests—or at least some of them. Our own contrast between the politics of rationality and the rationality of politics must be seen in this light. It is not merely party politicians who threaten to upset the rationalist's carefully arranged apple-cart, it is all actors—high or low—who exhibit a leaning towards *ad hoc* neigotiations, deals and opportunistic actions.

To characterise the rational planning of the 1970s as essentially a centralist dead hand on party and bureaucratic politics would be misleading. The tendency was discernible, but the practice was never sufficiently developed to have that outcome. Moreover, the trend towards centralisation was matched by a desire to achieve decentralised forms of coordination. The inner cities provided one notable, not to say notorious, example; the health and personal social services provided another. Both examples added a further piece to the coordination jigsaw: while centrally devised plans could aid coordination by providing a coherent framework, the need at the local level was for collaboration. It was seen to be necessary for local actors and organisations to rise above any minor differences of opinion and interest in order to pursue the common good of the local community in concert. Indeed, it is an abiding feature of the rationality game that people who can see many reasonable—and rational—reasons for differences of opinion and divergences of interest at their own level of operation tend to emphasize the rationality of collaboration at other levels (and fail to see why there should be barriers or obstacles in the path of such a self-evident good).

Centralisation is an inherently relative concept. What was perceived by central government as a valuable or even essential attempt to develop decentralised collaboration was often perceived by local actors and observers as further evidence of centralisation. Corporate planning in local government was a prime example. The attempt, initself laudable and long overdue, to achieve greater coordination across local government departments became inseparably entwined with the reorganisation of local government into much larger, more remote and more bureaucratically complex units. The same was true of collaboration between the health and personal social services. Moreover, the collaboration in question was between whole departments and organisations and was designed to promote another layer of rational planning. The term 'coordination' has warmer and more personal overtones then the term 'condination', but in practice it did not imply too many cosy chats about mutual interests—it merely entailed some attempt to harmonise the actions of large organisations characterised by divergent interests. As we shall illustrate from our own empirical work, it was generally as resolutely technical and technocratic (few local politicians played a decisive role) as the attempt at rational planning initiated within central government.

Nonetheless, these different developments highlighted a single and crucial issue: the large-scale state social services which had been developed in the post-war years could fail to meet—or could even exacerbate—people's needs, as well as resolve them. One central reason for this was that policies, the structure of service systems, and the actual delivery of services all exhibited gaps in coverage, conflicts of aim and failures of communication. Better coordination was the solution and it could take several forms (that there could possibly be other sources of failure and other potential solutions is a point to which we shall return).

The two forms of coordination which we have mentioned—rational planning and collaboration—require a further word of explanation. In one sense they represent the difference between technique and process. *Rational planning* is one technique by which a framework to guide and coordinate action can be achieved. Collaboration is a process of interaction in which two or more parties identify mutual interests and freely agree to work together towards a common goal. *Collaboration* is therefore one way of *developing* a rational plan, and it was seen to be a necessary way at the local level (because many autonomous agencies needed to work together and there was no acceptable means of coercing them to do so). By way of comparison, a second way of engaging in rational planning is for an acknowledged authority to require different groups and interests to submit to a single coherent strategy. *Imperative* (or coercive) and *collaborative* processes may both be involved in the process of rational planning, therefore, Government departments engaged in planning might do so through a combination of these processes. Ministers, cabinet and transdepartmental bodies [...] might exercise authority or persuasion, but much might also hinge upon unforced collaboration across sections, divisions and departments. [...]

However, we later use the term *collaboration arena* in a quite specific sense which should be distinguished now. It is used to refer to the field of local interaction between the health authorities, local authorities and voluntary agencies. Its use reflects the fact that central government policies have characterised coordination and joint planning at this level as *essentially* collaborative precisely because the organisations involved are autonomous of one another and, to varying degrees, of central government. Any plan of action agreed by such agencies would immediately take on a different role within those separate agencies—it would be authoritative—but it would itself be the product of purely collaborative interaction. In reality, joint planning has never been innocent of authoritative action by central departments. [...] Joint planning has been heavily mandated from above. Nonetheless, central government writ runs but imperfectly at such local levels and collaboration has remained the essential ingredient. Hence we use the term *collaborative arena* to specify joint planning between health and local authorities and voluntary bodies.

Even before 1979, no actuary would have taken a risk on the life expectancy of rational planning; the more grandiose hopes and ambitions had already begun to crumble and decay. Once the first Thatcher administration had come to power, it was only a matter of time before the life support machine was switched off altogether. What had finally disappeared, after a long period of false alarms, was the entire post-war tradition of consensus politics. Most fundamentally, the competence and role of the state had been re-evaluated and re-defined. State paternalism—and 'dirigiste' central planning—were anathema. Yet, as we have argued [...] the need for policy coordination has survived this dramatic change in political ideology. It has everywhere undergone a change of style or of name, it has on occasions gone underground, but in only a few cases has it gone out of the window. A considerable degree of continuity of practice has accompanied sharp changes in principle. What, then, is to be learned about coordination and the politics of rationality from the experiences of the early 1980s?

The first lesson is that a market-oriented philosophy throws a different light on the whole issue of rationality and coordination in the social policy field. It redefines the problems and highlights different potential solutions. Ideally, rational decision-making and coordination is left primarily to the individual consumer at the point of consumption. The emphasis, in principle, is on consumer choice between outputs rather than on political or bureaucratic decision-making and the coordination of inputs and policy processes. Consumers are expected to be able to put together their own package of social provisions. Coordination is still necessary if government is to create the right framework within which a mixed economy of statutory, voluntary or private producers can operate. It is also still necessary within and between statutory producers. But the weight of coordinative responsibility is decentralised somewhat and the parties covered by the coordinative imperative are different—coordination between public and private producers grows in importance.

The second lesson is that the 'rationality of politics' has been reasserted in a major way at the strategic leel. The tendency to depoliticize policy issues has been swept aside. What was always clear to many has become perfectly clear to all: rationality resides in the choice of means to ends, but the choice between ends is inherently political. Faith in consensus has been at a minimum; divergent and conflicting interests have come out of the closet. Yet this reassertion of the rationality of politics has been highly selective. It has been confined to the national tier of government and to 'high politics'. Neither differences of interest and viewpoint between centre and locality, nor bureaucratic politics, has been countenanced as a legitimate barrier to the implementation of key policies. Coordinated action has remained very much in demand once political decisions have been made: *instrumental* rationality has lost none of its appeal. It is any lingering belief in *substantive* rationality—a uniquely appropriate understanding of the public good whcih can be discerned through sophisticated policy analysis – which has disappeared from view.

A third, obvious but often overlooked, lesson has also been forcibly restated. The more grandiose formulations of the rational synoptic planning approach contained a deep-rooted paradox. They were an attempt to contain and discipline the *ad hoc* and short-term nature of purely political decision-making and yet they were fundamentally dependent on the support and commitment of politicians. [...] The British Civil Service is deeply conservative in its ways and resistant to implanted foreign bodies such as policy units and think-tanks; only civil service loyalty to committed ministers could offset the deleterious consequences of departmental and sectional loyalties for the vital organs of the rational approach. Ministerial support for synoptic planning was patchy and uncertain at best before 1979, but it ceased altogether thereafter.

Coordination: Components and Dimensions

Coordination remained a key aspect of the style of governance which characterised the early 1980s, but it was shorn of most of the trappings of rational planning. The issues to which it was seen to be most pertinent also changed. Public expenditure control moved sharply up the agenda, as did law and order and, more gradually, the link between education/training and 'manpower planning'. But what does coordination entail? What kind of phenomenon or process are we discussing? Now that the rhetoric and organisational machinery of the rational planning era have been jettisoned, it is somewhat easier to pereceive the essential elements. Coordination in social planning may refer to one or more of the following:

(a) ensuring consistency and coherence between the *various objectives and elements of a single policy or project;*
(b) ensuring consistency and coherence within a *set of interacting policies or projects* 'owned' by one or more departments ro organisations;
(c) ensuring that policy is translated into a consistent and coherent set of *appropriate actions* within one or more departments or organisations;

(d) ensuring that *service delivery practices* at the field level are such that a consistent, coherent and comprehensive package of help is available to people with specified needs;

(e) ensuring that the *services actually consumed* by the public in contact comprise a consistent, coherent and comprehensive package appropriate to expressed wants.

To begin with the last, we have noted that the market philosophy places considerable emphasis on coordination at this stage as a function of consumer choice. In a more traditional public service frame of analysis, this view of implementation implies the evaluation of outputs and outcomes from the consumer's perspective. The first four forms of coordination fit readily within the public service perspective: the first two emphasize coordination in policy-making, and the second two underline the importance of policy implementation. Both these 'levels' of coordination were covered in our empirical research. [...]

Coordination can also be specified in terms of the kinds of activities involved. Three distinctions are especially pertinent:

(a) coordination as a *cerebral or analytical activity* (e.g. establishing an appropriate mix of objectives and methods in a policy or project at the planning stage);

(b) coordination as the *interaction of formal organisations* (agencies or departments of a large organisation) *or groupings* (e.g. professions) and the possibly competing or conflicting interests which they contain or represent;

(c) coordination as the *interaction of individuals* – usually as representatives or members of organisations or groupings (e.g. politicians, chief officers, middle managers, professionals and other field workers).

Each of these facets of coordination presents different issues. The first was the jewel in the rational planning crown, though some account had necessarily to be taken of the second. However, the rational planning era did tend to obscure the importance of the second and third; they were less glamorous and also less amenable to centralised control through paper planning exercises. But for our own purposes they are central: the interactive elements of the coordination process were the key object of our empirical research.

Coordination can finally be characterised in terms of a series of dichotomies. Two of the most significant—*centralised/decentralised* and *authoritative/collaborative*—have already been mentioned. They are broadly indicative of important variables rather than precise specifications. The third—*formal/informal*—is similar in this respect. By formal we mean coordination attempted through official channels or special machinery (e.g. joint consultative committees); by informal we mean the interaction of individuals or small groups as representatives and as people. The latter introduces the human element: the importance of personalities and interpersonal interaction. As such it is pervasive. Interpersonal interaction may tip the balance in favour of a particular outcome within a highly formal committee meeting just as much as over a drink at the bar afterwards. We do not intend these dichotomies to be seen as mutually exclusive polarities, therefore. They are important dimensions of our analysis which are best summarised briefly in this manner for the time being.

The analytical component of coordination was explored at considerable length in a large body of academic writing before and during the rational planning era. Changes in the process of governance were strongly underpinned by theory. But they were also strongly criticised by alternative bodies of theory. Moreover, once the emphasis shifts from coordination as policy analysis to coordination as organisational interaction it is quite apparent that the body of academic writing which could be drawn upon as a guide to understanding is immense. Consequently, in developing guiding hypotheses for our research we had to be severely selective. We drew upon a wide range of literature, but concentrated on key ideas relating to the interactions which we most wanted to study and understand. It is to this academic framework that we must now turn.

Theories and Hypotheses

To begin to understand the approach take towards rationality in the 1970s one has only to look at the one comparatively coherent and manageable body of literature advocating rational synoptic planning, or—in later revisionist versions—mixed scanning. But there is also a need to understand the likely limits of and impediments to these routes to coordination, and the literatures in this case are altogether more diverse and intimidating. It is true that the rational planning literature was counterbalanced by the 'incrementalist school' which trenchantly criticised both the feasibility and desirability of the rational synoptic approach, but simply to draw on this would not be wholly appropriate. The image of a sharp antithesis between the 'rational planning' and 'incrementalist' schools was always overdrawn and resulted in fundamentally distinct issues being conflated. For example, the idea of incremental policy processes seemed to convey a single, coherent phenomenon, but incrementalism could, in fact, convey any or all of the following:

- the avoidance of grand strategies in favour of single-issue decision-taking;
- the avoidance of elaborate policy analysis in favour of political judgement and the 'intelligence of democracy';
- the avoidance of centralized policy-making in favour of more decentralized decision-taking.
- the avoidance of dramatic change in policy objectives in favour of more conservative patterns of change; and
- the acceptance of undramatic or conservative shifts in policy outputs at the expense of radical change.

Neither sophisticated analysis nor radical policies necessarily means radical changes in outputs (or vice versa), but these small matters of causality were often lost sight of in the partisan heat of a great academic debate. However, given the qualifications and intellectual disentangling which are now possible, the incrementalist literature obviously proved to be a valuable source of ideas and guiding hypotheses when first we began our research. Nonetheless, we faced a further problem. Both the rational synoptic planning literature and—to a lesser extent—the incrementalist rejoinder concentrated on 'high politics': on the nature of policy-making rather than on the whole politico-administrative process. We therefore needed to draw additional perspectives, especially on organisational interaction, into our theoretical net. We had also to identify a simple framework within which ideas from these various literatures could be marshalled.

Notwithstanding the dangers of over-generalising and of drawing unduly hard distinctions between literatures characterised by diversity and subtlety, two broad traditions of thought can certainly be discerned. We will label them, for convenience, the 'optimistic' and 'pessimistic' traditions. However, it is important to emphasize that we only present them as optimistic and pessimistic in relation to our chosen issue: the possibility and likelihood of achieving coordination as an expression and outcome of a wider commitment to rationality in public affairs.

The 'Optimistic' Tradition

The 'optimistic' tradition is characterised by persistence in the face of recurring disappointments; it follows a cyclical pattern of enthusiasm, disillusionment and resurrection. Its rhetoric is enduring because it evokes commitment to a particular way of viewing the world:

> The first of the shared commitments is to rationality. Coordination strategies carry an authoritative ring of technical competence and planning...The most obvious point is that integration of human services makes sense...A reform strategy that claims to bring order out of chaos becomes very appealing. There is a deep and pervasive vein of current conventional wisdom, namely that all things should be unified, quantified, ordered, consolidated and computerised... Unification is good, duplication is bad... official order is safe, pluralistic order is less than safe. Coordination appeals to this proposition.

In short, the 'optimistic' tradition survives because it reflects and embodies the ideology of public bureaucracies concerned to bring about predictability and regularity in a turbulent world. Without coordination there will be conflict or wasteful competition.

The primary focus of this tradition in recent times, apart from the process of rational synoptic planning itself, has been the organisational framework necessary for the survival of that process. Organisational dysfunction, as we have noted, was widely diagnosed as the major barrier to effective coordination throughout the 1960s and 1970s: organisational structures, formal machinery and planning processes were highlighted as the crucial prerequisities of progress. [...]

The prerequisites and assumptions entailed in the 'optimistic' tradition underline the organisational and behavioural demands and expectations which it involves. At minimum the idea of rational planning implies:

(a) a broad, system-wide perspective rather than a narrow or sectional view of problems, needs and issues;
(b) the existence, or achievement, of broad areas of consensus on goals, the nature of the problems to be tackled, the most acceptable and efficacious methods of intervention, and on priorities;
(c) a significant capacity for rational analysis, combined with authoritative backing;
(d) organisational arrangements appropriate to the analysis of problems and the implementation of solutions.

The assumption is that rational planning springing from such a conducive environment will provide the authoritative framework within which coordination will occur at all levels. As we have noted, the exception—a very major exception—arises from the frequent absence of imperative coordination: collaboration is necessary if policy and action are to be coordinated across the boundaries of autonomous organisations and groupings. However, collaboration, as Webb and Wistow have indicated, implies further and no less demanding requirements:

(a) that a system-wide perspective will pervade all organisations and groups which do, or which ought to, interact;
(b) that 'system-gain' (e.g. the greater good of the client or community) will be readily identified by all and will act as a sufficient reward for the achievement of consensus;
(c) that where pursuing system-gain conflicts with short-term and sectional interests, the latter will triumph—'organisational altruism' will be the order of the day.

The matter of organisational altruism is crucial precisely because the rational tradition underplays the power of divergent interests. It assumes that consensus is readily achievable and it has no solution to offer—other than authoritative action by a higher body—if it is not forthcoming. Given the reality of divergent sectional interests, collaborative rational action must therefore depend to some extent, possibly a major extent, on the altruistic willingness of organisations or groupings to forgo some of these sectional interests. It is one of the issues we clearly had to built into the hypotheses and propositions which guided our empirical research.

The 'Pessimistic' Tradition

While the rational tradition optimistically posits an underlying social harmony, the many alternative viewpoints are united precisely in their pessimism—or realism—on this point. The assumption is that 'harmony of needs is not only undiscoverable but non-existent'. In the tradition of Hayek and Popper, true rationality resides in process—the interplay of individual preferences and decisions—not in the imposition of a collective strategy. 'Pluralistic disorder' is positively embraced, or at the very least acknowledged. The notion of an overarching rationality is seen as a share and delusion leading to the 'preceptorial society'.

Beyond the prescriptive and tendentious elements of this perspective there is a central observation with which observers from all points of the ideological compass have been able to concur: individual and group interests are multiple and divergent, and the net result is competition, bargaining and conflict. As with the tradition of optimism about rationality, routes back to some form of relatively harmonious social order are typically sought and prescribed—whether in the classical liberal advocacy of the market or the classical Marxist advocacy of a wholly novel socioeconomic order. Nonetheless, theorists in the 'pessimistic' tradition begin by recognising divergent and conflicting interests and it is this preliminary observation which throws much light on the deficiencies, and indeed the potential dangers, of the search for a rational consensus in public affairs. Without a class or conflict perspective, for example, it would be much more difficult to highlight the enormous potential of 'coordination' as an instrument of neglect (benign or otherwise), of official evasion, or of repressive social control. But for the purposes of guiding our empirical research, a potentially vast literature which was explicitly or implicitly critical of the rational optimistic tradition had to be translated into a manageable number of insightful propositions and guiding hypotheses on three topics central to the coordination issue:

information;
the nature of policy; and
the nature of interaction between organisations.

Information: Coping with Overload

Failures of communication and pleas for better information exchange are perennial. They are the smokescreen for incompetence and bad faith, but also the time-honoured figleaf with which to disguise the unpalatable fact of divergent interests where harmony and rational collaboration are presumed to reign. However, even assuming that communication is the problem and not the scapegoat, the 'optimistic' tradition tends towards naivety. Information is treated as costless, as self-evidently good and as a force for unity rather than division. The alternative is to stress the costs of both generating and processing information, and the problems of coping with it.

The most familiar result of viewing information as problematic is to conclude, with Simon, that individuals and organisations will tend to 'satisfice' rather than 'optimise'. The rational model assumes that maximising information and analysis will maximise the quality of decision-making. That, in practice, the costs of pursuing perfect information are great is indisputable, but the argument can be taken further. For the individual actor learning to cope with a particular kind of information is an 'irreversible investment'; the 'code' has to be learned. For the organisation this process represents a significant accumulation of 'capital'; once created, therefore, organisations have distinct identities which are comparatively inflexible due to the costs involved in changing codes. The process of coping with information consequently erects barriers to coordination, especially to collaboration.

The more efficient an organisation (or profession) is in developing its own code – i.e. its way of handling and interpreting information – the more difficult it may be to communicate with other organisations. A similar conclusion is suggested by cognitive theory. Organisational actors develop analytical paradigms which allow them to cope with uncertainty and ambiguity in dealing with information. In Steinbruner's words, 'Pertinent information may enter the decision process or it may be screened out, depending on how it relates to the existing pattern of belief; information 'which is threatening to established belief pattern' may be rejected. This, in turn, may lead to 'grooved thinking': the organisational actor's decisions' are programmed so that once he determines which category obtains, the decision follows without further question'. This is first cousin to the notion of Standard Operating Procedures (SOPs), described as follows by Allison:

> Rules of thumb permit concerted action by large numbers of individuals, each responding to basic cues. The rules are usually simple enough to facilitate easy learning and unambiguous application. Since procedures are 'standard' they do not change quickly or easily. Without such standard procedures, it would not be possible to perform certain concerted tasks...Some SOPs are simply conventions that make possible regular or coordinated activity. But most SOPs are grounded in the incentive structure of the organisation or even in the norms of the organisation of the basic attitudes and operating style of its members. The stronger the grounding, the more resistant SOPs are to change.

Once again, the more efficient organisations are in developing their own analytic paradigms and SOPs—i.e. in coordinating their internal activities—the more difficult they may find it to enter into a dialogue with other organisations, since they will be using different organisational languages.

The problems of organisational information-handling raise some further questions about the assumptions made—if only implicitly—in the 'optimistic' rational model. If coordination is about information exchange (among other things), what actually is being exchanged, and by whom? One way of organising the collection of information within the organisation is through hierarchy: the information flows up the official lines of authority. But this, as Downs argues, introduces bias since 'all types of officials tend to exaggerate data that reflect favourably on themselves and to minimise those that reveal their own shortcomings'. Such bias introduces information distortion. Thus

Tullock calculated that if, in an organisation with seven levels, the average official screens out only half the data given him by his subordinates, the winnowing process would eliminate 94.8 per cent of the data originally gathered by the time the information reached the top of the office. Yet a central feature of coordination, as we discovered, is precisely that it depends both upon detailed understanding of the key issues at the level at which coordination is to occur and upon decision-making authority. The choice of personnel to discuss and negotiate new arrangements is therefore a perennial problem and a crucial determinant of outcomes.

Policy: A Misleading Concept

The very idea of policy implies a degree of orderliness, even consensus; a way forward has been agreed and delineated. In the social policy field, moreover, the term 'policy' is typically taken to refer to the specification of the needs which are to be met and the means by which this is to be achieved. The implication—widely reflected in official policy on the inner cities and on the care of the elderly and other 'priority client groups'—is that what is required is coordination between different policies, each of which is designed to meet one of an interlocking set of needs. The real problem of coordination is seen to lie at the interface between the major strands of social policy and the major service departments and agencies which enact them.

This is a wholly misleading picture and it is one which arises from the conceptualisation of policy as a coherent, relatively self-contained, complete and authoritative guide to future action. However, this misleading picture also arises from the tendency in the post-war decades to split social policy off from the rest of the body politic and to treat it as a hermetically sealed arena of state intervention coterminous with the departments and agencies of social policy. In reality, policy processes are altogether more complex and messy. The conflicts and power struggles which determine the *outcomes* of social policy (as opposed to the content of statements of objectives which are merely *inputs*) are to be located throughout the government system and not only in the 'social policy departments'.

One way of expressing some of this complex reality is by thinking, as Webb and Wistow suggest, in terms of *streams of policies* which interact, compete and conflict, rather than in terms of policies as discrete and authoritative blueprints. They argue that social policy outcomes are best seen as the good product of at least three streams of interacting policies:

1. *service, or output, policies* – which specify the social needs to be met and the choice of appropriate means and methods of intervention;
2. *resource policies* – which specify broad patterns of expenditure, detailed allocations between competing uses, and the dominant approaches taken to resource management (e.g. to maximise long-term cost-effectiveness or to minimise total expenditure in the short term);
3. *governance policies* – which specify the general view taken of the role of the state as well as the philosophy of management and control to be adopted within public authorities (e.g. centralisation or decentralisation, detailed intervention or *laissez-faire*).

To these can be added a fourth:

4. *fiscal policies* – which specify the general view taken on the level and structure of taxation to be aimed at as well as the specific tax 'subsidies', benefits or breaks which are to be permitted.

What this formulation immediately reveals is the importance of seeing policies as a means of *expressing* conflicting interests rather than as the product of conflict resolution. A policy to ease the lot of institutionalised mentally ill people which founders for lack of resources can only be seen in the rational 'optimistic' tradition as a failure of communication and coordination. But it may more accurately be understood as the triumph of one interest (expressed through resource allocation policies) over the interests of mentally ill people (expressed through a service policy). It is therefore essential to look for competition and conflict between policies and also to recognise the divergent value systems, goals, dominant interests; and informational codes which may underpin differences between various policy streams.

To turn this perception of conflicting interests on its head is to reveal another dimension of coordination: to achieve a particular outcome for a vulnerable and weak interest group such as the mentally ill will not only depend on coordinating different social service organisations and objectives. It will depend on the degree of coordination achieved across the service, resource and fiscal policy streams, which in turn will depend upon the adoption of a governance strategy designed to effect congruence between service goals and resource commitments. In short, coordination is not merely a neutral technique. It can be a crucial element of any strategy to overcome—or to enhance—the bias in favour of dominant interests and ideologies which is inherent in our—and every—system of government. Coordination is itself about power and the purposeful use of power.

Power-Dependence and Organisational Interaction

The rational tradition tends to assume that the guiding ideology of public service organisations is the pursuit of the common good. One of the popular alternative viewpoints is that organisational actors are self-interested 'utility maximizers':

> Bureaucratic officials in general have a complex set of goals including power, income, prestige, security, convenience, loyalty (to an idea, an institution, or the nation), pride in excellent work, and desire to serve the public interest...But regardless of the particular goals involved, every official is significantly motivated by his own self-interest.

This view of organisational actors as economic men who will weigh up the costs and benefits to themselves of any given course of action, sensitizes us to incentives and disincentives to coordination (or any other desired objective). [...]

Viewing public service organisations as bodies dedicated to protecting their resource base (as distinct from necessarily seeking to maximise their budgets) has some further implications. It suggests that such organisations will seek to mobilise political support for their activities—and budgets—just as private sector business firms will seek to attract customers for their products. After all, in a period of resource stress even support for baseline activities cannot be taken for granted. Such support mobilisation strategies may take a variety of forms, but one self-evident strategy consists of proclaiming the organisation's special and unique role in protecting the interests or well-being of a popular or politically strong client group. To establish a monopoly of care or provision for such a group is to assert the claim that any attack on the organisation—such as budget retrenchment—is also an attack on those clients. In a sense, popular clients are valuable property, to be defended against other, competing organisations. Conversely, of course, one might expect public sector organisations to be less interested in the care of less popular client groups. Willingness to collaborate would, therefore, be most unlikely where one organisation see itself as having established a desirable monopoly and most likely where a client group is seen as marginal to the agency's main role or as imposing burdens which do not bring in any compensatory inputs of support. In this respect, the rational strategy for public sector organisations would be similar to that for professions, in so far as the process of professionalisation can be seen as the assertion of monopoly control over certain social functions or skills (a conclusion which would, in turn, suggest that a public sector organisation containing a strong professional element would have a double incentive to warn possible competitors off its policy patch). [...]

The rational perspective draws heavily on Weber and a host of modern interpreters united by the basic tenets of the classic theory of bureaucracy, but alternative viewpoints spring from a variety of disciplinary perspectives and often lack even a common vocabulary. Nonetheless, a central theme is the insistence on viewing organisations as 'bargaining and influence systems'. If individual actors seek to maximise utilities, groups and even whole organisations can be understood in the same terms. Organisations compete for resources with the result that the normal mode of co-existence is not harmonious collaboration but bargaining, power play and conflict.

Lindblom's early contribution to the debate rested on the assumption that organisations would coordinate their activities only if it was in their own Self-Interest; attempts at exhortation or at establishing formal coordinative machinery would not be likely to have much effect. Lindblom's approach was consistent with a heterogeneity of literature sailing under the flag of exchange theory. One of its great merits is that it identifies many of the barriers and opportunities which shape bargaining processes. The starting point is that bargaining, or exchange, is a function of interdependence: interdependent organisations 'must take each other into account if they are to accomplish their goals'.

Interdependence consists of interlocking patterns of demand and supply for resources; material resources such as capital, income flows, labour and clients, but also less tangible resources such as information, expertise, authority and the capacity to authorise. Bargaining depends upon complementary patterns of demand and supply for such resources and also upon the likelihood of substituting readily available alternative for needed resources possessed exclusively by a rival organisation. [...]

Aiken and Hague have argued that for bargaining and exchange to take place 'there must be some slack in the resource base'. Subsequent empirical findings suggested that scarcity may provide the motive but that 'those agencies most willing to act upon this motive are those relatively rich in clients and non-human resources'. The obvious proposition—which informed our own choice of empirical research sites—is that a finely balanced experience of pressure and comparative security (or room for manoeuvre) provides the strongest spur to exchange through bargaining.

However, the picture is further complicated by the transaction costs involved in inter-organisational exchange. Negotiation ties down staff and involves uncertainty and risks. These costs may in turn depend upon the networks if any, which link organizations. As thrasher has argued, 'networks' which persist over time are likely to exhibit different exchange patterns than those which are newly created. The need to create networks and engender trust can be a major transaction cost. What this suggests is that formal machinery may have no relevance where the preconditions for bargaining are absent, but it may play a real role in giving permanence to networks and lowering transaction costs.

The importance of networks underlines the fact that the rewards sought on behalf of organisations and those sought by their representatives as individuals differ. Individual actors may aspire to many non-material rewards: status, social approval and friendship. Nonetheless, the individual actor, just as much as the organisation, is viewed essentially as self-interested rather than altruistic.

To recognise networks and diverse non-material rewards is to accept that exchange and bargaining constitute a complex social game which is likely to be played according to rules—rules which define socially acceptable behaviour and transactions.

Relationships between organisations, groupings and policy streams may be based on competition and conflict rather than on consensus, but competition and conflict are constrained by 'basic rules of conduct'. Moreover, interlocking it ansactions may take place in more than one arena: 'some resources gained in one arena may be used to win prizes in anaother arena'.

The complexity of the bargaining relationships through which policies and actions may become more (or less) coordinated points to two crucial issues for empirical research: the structuring of arenas by government and the role of 'middlemen'. The first of these is summarised in Webb and Wistow's phrase, 'the structuring of local policy environments'. Health and local authorities, for example, do not relate one to another in a vacuum. Central government systematically, though not necessarily intentionally, influences the resources needed by and available to these organisations. It structures the formal organisational arrangements which impinge on the development of networks of relationships, and it determines many of the costs and benefits of interaction. It may also affect the availability of 'middlemen'. [...]

The superficial attractions of the rational 'optimistic' tradition are even clearer when it is remembered that stable patterns of exchange and bargaining rest upon a broad symmetry between organisations and a recognition that opportunities exist for rewarding exchange. The first is crucial not least because it raises the ghost at this feast: power. Bargaining and exchange arise from dependence: a wholly independent organisation with no pressing unmet resource needs can afford to go its own way without reference to others. But dependence bestows power on the resource-rich party; undue dependence implies dominance by another. Reasonably symmetrical patterns of dependence are therefore the stimulus to exchange. Moreover, a symmetrical pattern of dependence has to be *perceived.* Opportunities for exchange which go unnoticed, and exchange possibilities which are seen to include unduly high costs, or risks of dominance, will simply result in non-interaction—even the active avoidance of interaction. [...]

The obvious caveat which must be appended to this power-dependence/bargaining-exchange model of organisational interaction is that power may be too narrowly conceived. Wrong suggested the narrowness of the approach taken by arguing: 'I do not see how we can avoid restricting the term 'power' to intentional and effective control by particular agents'. Emerson, even more specifically, asserted: 'The power of A over B is equal to, and based upon the dependence of B upon A. These views of power could be stretched to include all that we would wish to include, but it is better by far to follow Lukes and adopt a more catholic formulation. The kind of power most readily incorporated within the approach suggested by Wrong and Emerson and many others, is essentially overt – it is a behavioural approach to power. It comprises what Bachrach and Baratz called the first face of power. In their terms, the second face of power added another ingredient: non-decisions. This concept has been greatly ill-used, but Bachrach and Baratz applied in situations in which possible lines of action or behaviour were intentionally excluded from discussion, or were kept off the agenda, by power-holders. To take an example, a highly self-sufficient organisation may perennially disregard calls to coordinate its actions with those of a less powerful organisation; an arrogant insularity may keep the coordination issue off the agenda altogether. [...]

From the point of view of central government departments seeking to encourage coordination in social policy, the 'pessimistic' tradition of academic analysis makes dismal reading. The central government tendency has always been to rely on the rational model. Organisations and professions are exhorted to look beyond their sectional interests and to work together for the greater good of clients and the community. Such altruism is expected to be its own reward. The 'pessimistic' academic tradition underlines all the barriers not only of self-interest *per se,* but of exceedingly complicated patterns of self-interest. Interaction may occur through bargaining and exchange and it may possibly lead to desired patterns of coordination. But it may, even more plausibly, lead to no such thing. Organisational relationships, where they occur, may fall far short of such well-developed exchanges. Partisan mutual adjustment, to use Lindblom's old expression, may merely involve organisations in changes of practice which are designed to avoid or minimise conflict. It may facilitate unilateral development, which Glennerster identifies as the dominant contemporary mode of action in the social policy field. rather than presaging close collaboration. Unilateral change by one organisation to accommodate the policies of another may produce desired coordination, or it may merely represent two ships of state passing in the night.

While non-interaction and failures of coordination may be the most readily explained phenomena, the 'pessimistic' tradition does hold out hope of more concerted action. It points to the possibility of systematically structuring arenas so that they facilitate and promote collaborative exchange. The conditions may be demanding and government action may need to be finely tuned if it is to succeed, but the message—in essence—is simply that 'policy implementation' ought to be as central and as well informed a feature of government as 'policy-making'. That opportunities for concerted influence do exist is the optimistic part of the 'pessimistic' tradition from a governmental point of view.

What is also apparent is that these academic perspectives are substantially complementary, rather than in conflict. The great rational synoptic planning versus incrementalism debate obscured this complementarity. An emphasis on power-dependence and bargaining needs to be balanced by reference to the possibility—however slight—that social service organisations and professions may at times take a broad, altruistic view and elevate system (or client) gain above sectional interests. However, to speak of altruism in this context could be misleading, for it is the value base and service ethos of the social services which may produce such a 'rational' outcome. If government neglects to build and mobilise such a value base, it is indeed relying upon pure altruism to generate collaboration.

Similarly, the 'pessimistic' emphasis on processes of interaction, bargaining and conflict is needed to balance frequent references to structures. The elegant mansion of rational synoptic planning was constructed without sufficient regard to the need for adequate foundations or to the problems of managing a large and disputatious household. Nonetheless, it did at least recognise that walls and roof are more likely to join, and skilled workers are more likely to be brought together, when everyone has a blueprint in their hands. Neither the emphasis on structure nor that on planning is irrelerant: together they may, as we have argued, provide the context in which networks develop and flourish—networks which are vital to processes of interaction. [...]

2

Goals of Management

PETER DRUCKER: Frances, of all the new programs you have successfully introduced into your 335 Girl Scout Councils around the country in thirteen years as National Executive Director, which is the one closest to your heart?

FRANCES HESSELBEIN: I would have to say the Daisy Scouts. This is our newest program for little girls, five years old or in kindergarten. In partnership with our Girl Scout Councils, we studied the needs of girls and we studied the American family in all of its configurations, and concluded that girls who are five years old are quite ready for a program working in a small group with two sensitive leaders. In this country today 85 percent of all children five years old are in school all or part of the day.

PETER DRUCKER: That was quite a departure, wasn't it, from the Girl Scout tradition?

FRANCES HESSELBEIN: Yes. Previously, we served girls from seven through seventeen. We moved the Brownie age level back to six because it was very clear as we studied the needs of girls that Brownies were ready at six. It became equally clear that young girls of five were ready for a Girl Scout program designed just for them.

PETER DRUCKER: Were your Councils enthusiastic about the change?

FRANCES HESSELBEIN: I'm afraid that only 70 of the 335 were enthusiastic, wanted to move right then. We had another thirty in the wings thinking more positively about it. But we began with one third of our Councils on board.

PETER DRUCKER: Am I right that you can't order the Councils to do anything?

FRANCES HESSELBEIN: The Councils are chartered, and they have their own volunteer board of directors. They work to meet the special needs of girls in their own areas. So in this case, they really had a choice—move with us or stand back and wait.

PETER DRUCKER: Quite a few of your Councils were, to say the least, dubious, am I right?

FRANCES HESSELBEIN: Yes, they were. But when we were ready to move with the training of the trainers and leaders of Daisy Girl Scouts, we had almost two hundred Girl Scout Councils ready, enthusiastic, and able to open their doors to these newest members.

PETER DRUCKER: How long did it take to go from seventy to two hundred Councils?

FRANCES HESSELBEIN: That took about six months. Within a year the Daisy Scouts were established as one of our most successful endeavors. Three years later, the Daisy Scouts were everywhere in this country. Councils discovered they can offer leadership positions to young women and older women who were reluctant to work with teenagers but who find working with five-year-olds an adventure.

PETER DRUCKER: How many Daisy Scouts do you have now?

FRANCES HESSELBEIN: Approximately 150,000—and growing fast.

PETER DRUCKER: So let me try to play back what I think you told me. First, you were market-driven. You went out and looked at the needs, the wants of the community you serve, and they had changed since you first started seventy-five years ago. So you developed this service that was market-driven. Next, you have to market, you have to persuade, you have to create customers for the new mission because 335 Councils don't have to take a program just because you in New York say so. And the next thing I think you told us is that to make the change, you looked for what I call targets of opportunity—the Councils who really wanted this and were ready to go to work. You didn't worry about the Councils that were non-believers.

FRANCES HESSELBEIN: We began with those Councils ready and eager to move ahead with a new program for five-year-olds. Those not on the sled could wait. We made it very clear that they had a choice. But we were firm in our determination to move ahead with those who were ready and enthusiastic.

PETER DRUCKER: What about those who were ready but not competent?

FRANCES HESSELBEIN: Everyone who wanted to begin the program had to take the new training for trainers and for leaders. We never begin this kind of program without the adult education those women and men needed.

PETER DRUCKER: You said something terribly important. I've seen so many first-rate non-profit services fail because they were just offered, instead of the non-profit's managers making sure that everybody who has to do something knows what has to be done, is trained to do it, has the tools. Did you give your Councils the tools to bring in the new volunteers for this new program?

FRANCES HESSELBEIN: Yes, We created a wonderful handbook for Daisy Scout leaders. We made clear that there should be six to eight girls and at least two leaders in each group. The program had to be educationally sound. Then it had to be carried out in a way that was supportive and helpful. And we have been stressing that the leadership should come from the widest spectrum, not just the mother of the young girl, but young business and professional women. And moving to the other end, older

Americans, retired, with lots of energy and interest and willingness to help. I believe this has brought the kind of success, the kind of inclusiveness that is necessary if you're building a large volunteer workforce.

PETER DRUCKER: So you basically spent as much time on thinking through what the program has to be to attract volunteers as you spent on making the program fit the five-year-olds?

FRANCES HESSELBEIN: Yes. Not only the recruitment and placement of volunteers, but designing the training for them to meet their very special needs so that as they moved into work with their group of Daisy Scouts, they could feel very secure.

PETER DRUCKER: How much training does that mean?

FRANCES HESSELBEIN: It would depend upon the person. The staff and volunteers working with potential leaders are very sensitive about their readiness. Training is designed especially for them.

PETER DRUCKER: Now let's switch to another of your successful programs. You have been able to increase the number of volunteers at a time when your traditional volunteer has—I wouldn't say disappeared, but become mighty scarce because many young women no longer sit at home waiting for husbands to come home from work.

FRANCES HESSELBEIN: As we looked at the large core of volunteers, women and men, we realised that they deserved and required superior learning opportunities. Peter, do you remember how we brought the Volunteer Presidents of Girl Scout Councils to California where you gave a seminar on non-profit management? On the other coast we had a team of Harvard Business School faculty give a similar course to the executive directors of our Girl Scout Councils. The quality of those opportunities said something to the volunteers about how this organisation needed and respected them and their potential and gifts.

PETER DRUCKER: But how did you get those potential volunteers in the first place?

FRANCES HESSELBEIN: You can't recruit local volunteers from an office in New York. It has to be people in the community who really believe in the mission, who really care about girls, who go out and talk person-to-person with potential volunteers. Our 335 Girl Scout Councils have done a superb job of this.

PETER DRUCKER: Let me try to convert this into general ideas, concepts, and rules. You look at the volunteers as your most important market simply because the number of volunteers you can bring in determines how many girls you can serve. And you make a determined, continued effort to find the right people. Then you treat them, not as volunteers but as unpaid members of the organisation. You determine their job, you set the standard, you provide the training, and you basically set their sights high.

That, in my experience, is the secret to the crucial marketing problem of so many non-profit organisations—the volunteer professionals who get their satisfaction out of their work, not the paycheck.

FRANCES HESSELBEIN: You forgot one point—the recognition. It is important that someone says: "Thank you very much, you've made a major contribution." And this too is an important part of the support and care of that volunteer workforce.

PETER DRUCKER: Would the same approach, the same principles, apply to work in the minority communities, where you are more successful than, I would say, any other community service organisation in this country?

FRANCES HESSELBEIN: One of the priorities of our National Board of Directors and Girl Scout Councils has been, and is, offering equal access to membership to every girl in the United States. It is important as we reach out to girls in every racial and ethnic group to understand the very special needs, the culture, the readiness of each group. We know that we must find leaders there, whether it is a community of newly arrived Vietnamese or an older, established black community.

PETER DRUCKER: When you took over, the minority membership was small, wasn't it?

FRANCES HESSELBEIN: It was certainly small. The change required daily hard work. It's not enough to have a campaign zoom into a minority community, recruit people, and leave. It requires the most thoughtful kind of planning and including those community leaders in that planning.

PETER DRUCKER: Well, give me an example.

FRANCES HESSELBEIN: In a housing project there are hundreds of young girls, really needing this kind of program, families wanting something better for their children. We work with clergymen, perhaps, with the director of that housing project, with parents—a group of people from that particular community. We recruit leaders, train them right there. In our recruitment brochure we have to demonstrate our respect for that community, our interest in it. Parents have to know that it will be a positive experience for their daughters.

PETER DRUCKER: But what makes you go to that housing project or to that Vietnamese community in the first place?

FRANCES HESSELBEIN: We look at the projections and understand that by the year 2000, one third of this country will be members of minority groups. We have the most remarkable opportunity to serve in new ways. We have to understand what this means to a local Girl Scout Council with many changing ethnic and racial groups within its jurisdiction. To really give leadership to this and to be ready for the year 2000, we developed a national center for innovation. We have a highly skilled staff moving in first to Southern California, where the change is coming so rapidly, working with a small group of Southern Californian Councils, developing models of how a council reaches out to all the girls in its council boundaries and how we really provide that equal access which is so essential.

PETER DRUCKER: Those seven California Councils are already about 30 percent minority populations, right? So that you are actually working on the target of opportunity. They know they need the help. And you also demonstrate effect. If it works here, it's going to work in Buffalo.

FRANCES HESSELBEIN: We chose California. It is the bellwether state, in our opinion, and these models then can be adapted wherever Councils in this country are faced with the opportunity of serving diverse and rapidly changing populations. Theory is not enough.

In 1912, our founder said, "I have something for all the girls." We take this very seriously. Many people are very apprehensive about the future and what this new racial and ethnic composition will mean to our country. We see it as an unprecedented opportunity to reach all girls with a program that will help them in their growing-up years, which are more difficult than ever before.

PETER DRUCKER: Frances, isn't it pretty typical of the nonprofit organisation that it has more than one customer? You, for instance, have the girls, but also the volunteers.

FRANCES HESSELBEIN: I believe it is typical. Rarely does a nonprofit organisation have "a" customer. If we market to only one of our customers, I think we fail.

PETER DRUCKER: And what would your general conclusions be about introducing a new program?

FRANCES HESSELBEIN: You must carefully construct a marketing plan. Not just disseminate information about it, but understand all the ways there are to reach people and use them. Distributing written materials isn't enough. You need people in the marketing chain. And there has to be continuing evaluation—getting feedback on how we are doing. And if a strategy is not working regroup and move ahead in a different way.

3

Strategies for Success

There is an old saying that good intentions don't move mountains; bulldozers do. In non-profit management, the mission and the plan – if that's all there is – are the good intentions. Strategies are the bulldozers. They convert what you want to do into accomplishment. They are particularly important in non-profit organisations. One prays for miracles but works for results, St. Augustine said. Well, strategies lead you to work for results. They convert intentions into action and business into work. They also tell you what you need to have by way of resources and people to get the results.

I was once opposed to the term "Strategy." I thought that it smacked too much of the military. But I have slowly become a convert. That's because in many businesses and non-profit organisations, planning is an intellectual exercise. You put it in a nicely bound volume on your shelf and leave it there. Everybody feels virtuous: We have done the planning. But until it becomes actual work, you have done nothing. Strategies, on the other hand, are action-focused. So, I've reluctantly accepted the word because it's so clear that strategies are not something you *hope* for; strategies are something you *work* for.

Here is one example of a winning strategy: Brown University in Providence, Rhode Island. Twenty years ago it was a respectable "also ran", known as "harvard's little sister." It had an excellent faculty. But it had no distinction; it did what everybody else did. Then a new president asked, what do we have to do to become a leader despite the tough competition where we have Harvard to the north and Yale to the south, and about twelve first-rate liberal great many, but quite a few. But with paranoia, there are very limited results." He answered, "You are wrong, Peter. We have a simple goal. We know we don't know how to cure it; we don't understand it at all. But there is a possibility of helping people who are sick with paranoia to realise that they are sick. And that is a tremendous step forward. Because then they know that *they* are sick, not that the world is sick. They are not cured, but they function."

That's a qualitative goal. You can set goals that are not measurable but can be appraised and can be judged.

The people in a really successful research laboratory cannot quantify their research results ahead of time. But they can sit down every three years and ask, What have we contributed in the last three years that did make a difference? And what do we plan to contribute? These are qualitative measures. And they are just as important as the quantitative ones. Let me say that you have to define quality first. Quantity without quality is the worst thing and will result in total failure.

And how does a pastor set a strategy? First, the pastor has to define the goals. What is he or she trying to do? Sure, you make certain assumptions about people if you are a pastor. You make the assumption that it probably increases their chance of salvation if they do go to church.

As an old schoolmaster, which I've been for sixty years, I assume that the longer kids sit on their backsides, the more they learn. These are not testable assumptions, but you've got to make them. So the pastor sets his or her goal, which is to build a congregation.

What kind of a congregation? Not every pastor has the same vision. You may find people who say, I just bring them to church; that's that's the main goal. The next one will say, No, I only want to bring certain kinds of people in. Both are in the same profession, but see their mission quite differently. One sees it as to build a broad base; the other wants to start a small community of true believers who will stand fast at Armageddon.

Then you have to ask What are the specific results I want? Whether it's a church or a hospital or a Boy Scout troops or a public library, your strategy will have the same structure. First, you need the goal, and it's got to fit your mission. But it also has to fit the environment in which you work. Then you think through specific results for specific areas. The pastor who sees his or her church in terms of large masses of parishioners segments the market and designs a service for each segment. I once sat in on a meeting at which a very successful pastor said: "Any fool who is ordained can build a large church in five to seven years if he focuses on five market segments. He has a youth ministry, a singles ministry, a young-married ministry, a home ministry for the shut-ins, and a ministry for the elderly. The rest is hard work." Then he added, "Of course, the targets you set for these five depend on the community you are in."

That's perhaps a little oversimplified, but I've heard hospital administrators talk very similarly. Look at the ultimate beneficiaries—call them the market—the ultimate clients. Whether that market is a church, a hospital, a Boy Scout troop, or a public library, you have the same structure for your strategy. If you are a public library, you have adults, young people, and preschoolers, and you serve the schools. I think of each of these groups as a separate market—they share a building, they share common services, they share a lot of books; but I think you go after them separately. And you develop a marketing plan. You will need money, and will have to allocate it sensibly. You will have to communicate and you will have to have feedback.

First, the goal must be clearly defined. Then that goal must be converted into specific results, specific targets, each focused on a specific audience, a specific market area. You may need a great many such specific strategies. The American Heart Association divides the American public from which it, raises money into fortyone different segments. That's quite a lot. But it explains perhaps why they have been so successful.

Next, you will need a marketing plan and marketing efforts for each target group. How are you really going to reach this specific *segment*? You now need *resources*—people, above all—and money. And the *allocation* of both.

Next comes *communication*—lots of it—and *training*. Who has to do what, when, and with what results? What tools do they need? In what language do they have to hear it? One pastor told me that when he sits down with each of his groups and talks about goals and missions, even after twenty-five years, he still uses the language of the seminary. But the people who have to do the work are his lay volunteers, and to them these are strange words. Words like 'implementation', 'fulfillment', and 'plan' when used by a hospital administration may sound strange, too, for somebody in physical therapy who knows all the muscles of the body. You have to ask who must do what, and in what form they should get it so that it becomes *their* works.

Then you need *logistics*—for want of a better word. What *resources* are required. I'm always reminded of the old story that whenever Napoleon's brilliant marshals came out with great plans of moving against Prussia, or Spain, or what have you, Napoleon would listen silently and then ask, "How many horses does it require?" Usually they hadn't thought it through and their plan outran the available horses. That's very typical.

Finally, you ask: "When do we have to see results?" Try not to be impatient. But you must be able to see whether you are on course when the results come in. *What feedback do you need? How do you measure your achievement* so that you realise that in this area, which is crucial, we are way behind our timetable? If we can't speed it up, we will have to scale everything back (the horses aren't there, in Napoleon's terms). Or, here we are ahead of our timetable? Is this an opportunity for us to speed it all up, or does it indicate that we are getting dangerously out of line? You need *feedback and control points.*

I think the steps are the same for every organisation. How you carry them out depends very much on what kind of an organisation you are.

To carry out the process, you need to use *both written and verbal communication.* A written process has the great advantage that you can hand out a sheet to everybody, go down the line, check it off, and say, "Any questions on point three?" And somebody says, "Are we on point three? I thought we were still on point two." You talk about it. Above all, you invite questions.

But you also have to encourage people to come back and say, "This is what I heard. Am I right that you expect me to do this?" That is much better done in *speaking* than in writing. Partly because there is *less misunderstanding* and partly because *it's freer* and *less formal.*

To my mind, the best example of a winning strategy in a non-profit institution is that of the Nature Conservancy. Its clear goal is to preserve as much as possible of God's ecological diversity of flora and fauna, which is endangered by man. The board members developed one strategy to find the places that needed preserving;

another to get the money to buy them; and a third to manage it. The market—the people from whom they get the money—is local. So they built state organisations that reach the local people, and a goal of, I believe, fifteen of these major nature preserves per year, which is very ambitious. They are meeting it because they were so clear about that goal and its implementation. I think that accounts for success pretty much across the board.

But there is one *don't* on strategy. Don't avoid defining your goals because it might be thought "controversial." This strategy almost destroyed a major hospital, which attempted to brush under the rug one tough and highly controversial question: Are we trying to fill as many of our beds as possible, or are we trying to deliver the best patient care Their best-known eye doctors had proposed to move eye surgery into a free-standing ambulatory eye clinic, next door to the hospital. The eye surgeons saw this as improving patient care, indeed, as the first step toward the healthcare delivery system of tomorrow; and so did some of the hospital administrators. But the board saw only that this move would cut bed occupancy, which was their first priority. Eventually, the prominent eye surgeons got tired of the wrangle and left the hospital altogether, taking with them their patients, both ambulatory and bed patients. Other prominent physicians followed. Three years later the hospital had gone downhill so much—both in reputation and in occupancy rate—that it had to sell out to a for-profit chain.

With strategy, one always makes compromises on implementation. But one does not compromise on goals, does not pussy-foot around them, does not try to serve two masters.

Here is another *don't:* Don't try to reach different market segments with the same message. Some years ago I helped develop an executive management program. We were crystal-clear on the goal; but we did not really spend enough time thinking through the market segments. We tried to sell the program to everybody the same way. After six or seven years of working very hard and not getting very far, we sat down and said, "look, we really have three quite separate markets. They may all belong in the same program, but they are coming for different reasons." We organised it to the point that we now have different administrators for these groups. And it works.

How to Innovate

Usually, there is no lack of ideas in non-profit orgnaisations. What's more often lacking is the willingness and the ability to convert those ideas into effective results. What is needed is an innovative strategy. The successful non-profit organisation is organised for the new—organised to perceive opportunities. Innovative organisations systematically look both outside and inside for clues to innovative opportunities.

One strategy is practically infallible: Refocus and change the organisation *when you are successful*. When everything is going beautifully. When everybody says, "Don't rock the boat. If it ain't broke, don't fix it." At that point, let's hope, you have some character in the organisation who is willing to be unpopular by saying, "Let's *improve* it." If you don't improve it, you go downhill pretty fast.

The great majority of major institutions that have gotten into real trouble over the last fifteen years are successes that rested on their laurels. Look at the American Labour Union in the early Eisenhower years. It was king of the jungle. But where is it now? The main reason for these calamities is that the people who said then, "We have obtained our objectives; now let's improve on them", were forced out. They were treated like the little boy who says a dirty word in church. Sears, Roebuck twenty years ago was the merchant prince, the first choice of seventy percent of American families. It became so complacent that it ignored all signs of change in the American marketplace. When you are successful is the very time to ask, "Can't we do better?" The best rule for improvement strategies is to put your efforts into your successes. Improve the areas of success, and change them.

The responsibility for this rests at the top, as in everything that has to do with the *spirit* of an organisation. And so the executives who run innovative organisations must train themselves to look out the window, to look for change. The funny thing is, it's easier to learn to look *out* the window than to look *inside*, and that's also a smart thing to do systematically.

The most successful college I know has managed—at a time of shrinking student population—to increase the number of its applicants and improve the quality of those applicants by just such a discipline. The president and the director of admissions spend alternate weeks visiting high schools and inquiring about the changing expectations of the kids. The pastoral church which is such a significant sociological phenomenon in today's America looks at changes in demographics, at all the young, professional, educated people who have been divorced from their background and need a community, need help, comfort, and spiritual sustenance. The change outside is an opportunity. You can force yourself to drive a different route to work; you can force yourself to sit down and talk with students, who are still in high school but thinking of college. You can force yourself to look at demographics—and that's your first source.

Then you look *inside* your organisation and search for the most important clue pointing the way to change: generally, it will be the unexpected success. Most organisations feel that they deserve the unexpected success and congratulate themselves on it. Very few see it as a call to action. My best story on this score is not an American story, it's from India, which has converted itself in less than twenty years from chronic famine to food surplus. One of the keys to this change was the unusual success of a large farm cooperative that had become the sales agent for a cheap European bicycle with an auxiliary motor. The only trouble was the farmers didn't want it; they didn't buy it. Amazingly enough, while orders for bicycles didn't come in, orders for *replacement* motors for bicycles the farmers hadn't bought came in by the bushel. Everybody said, "Those stupid farmers, don't they know they need a bicycle?" Except for one co-op official. He went out and asked, "What are you doing with them?" Well, he found that the farmers were using that little single-stroke gasoline engine as a motor for irrigation pumps, which had always been powered by hand. Perhaps the greatest single contribution to India's tremendous agricultural success is the gasoline irrigation pumps that now bring available water to where it's needed.

The first requirement for successful innovation is to look at a change as a potential opportunity instead of a threat.

Everybody is worried about the "latchkey kids." But for the Girl Scouts of the U.S.A., the fact that there are so many young girls today whose mothers are out at work became a tremendous opportunity that led to the creation of the Daisy Scouts. Faced with a change, we should always ask, How can this give us a chance to contribute?

The second question is, who in our organisation should really work on this? That's a crucial question. Most new things need to be incubated. They need to be piloted by somebody who really wants that innovation, who wants it to grow, who believes in it. Everything new also gets into trouble, so look for somebody who really wants to commit himself or herself and who has enough standing in the organisation.

Then think through the proper marketing strategy. What are you really trying to do? When you look at successful businesses, they have very different strategies. A company like Procter & Gamble has always had one clear strategy in bringing out a product: to be the first, and to dominate the market. If it works, that's a winning strategy; but it's terribly risky. For fifty years, IBM never has brought out a new product; it has always been a creative imitator. It also always aimed at market dominance, but it lets somebody else go in first because the first version is likely not to be quite right. The Japanese strategy is very different. It exploits the mistakes of the leaders, their bad habits, especially their arrogance.

Look into the possibility of developing a niche. One very successful non-profit hospital group does not develop community hospitals but examines what each local community needs. In one community there is room for a psychiatric hospital, in another room for a good gerontology center. Each is a specialty hospital. That is a strategy: if you come out with a speciality, don't try to do everything for everybody.

The Common Mistakes

There are a few common mistakes in doing anything new:

One is to go from idea into full-scale operation. Don't omit *testing* the idea. Don't omit the pilot stage. If you do, and skip from concept to the full scale, even tiny and easily correctible flaws will destroy the innovation.

But also don't go by what "everybody knows" instead of looking out the window. What everybody knows is usually twenty years out of date. In political campaigns, the ones who look so promising at the beginning and then fizzle out are usually the ones who go by what they believe everybody knows. They haven't tested it, and it turns out that "This was twenty years ago."

The next most common mistake is righteous arrogance. Innovators are so proud of their innovation that they are not willing to adapt it to reality. It's an old rule that everything that's new has a different market from the one the innovator actually expected. I remember one of my pastoral friends saying of a new program: "Great, a wonderful program for the newly married." The program was indeed a success. But to the consternation of the young assistant pastor who had designed it and ran it, not a single newly married couple enrolled in it. All the participants were young people who were living together and wondering whether they should get married. And as the senior pastor told me, he had a terrible time with his brilliant young assistant, who became righteous and said, "We haven't designed it for them." He wanted to throw them out.

Another common mistake is to patch up the old rather than to go all-out for the new. The present plight of General Motors clearly shows that in that case you will get only the costs of the new, and none of its benefits. When the Japanese came in and the American public changed its approach to the automobile, GM patched. GM improved a little bit what it already was doing, and spent enormous amounts of money and time and people on patching—far more than genuine innovation would have required. A few years later Ford ran around GM. Ford sat down and said, "What does the new require?" It designed new cars and new ways of selling them, and risked a good deal of existing investment. But Ford brought out something that looked and behaved differently, and that could really compete.

There comes a point when one has to look at what the job requires, and design for that job, rather than saying, "This is how we've always done it. Let's improve it a little bit." This is one of the critical decisions. It is one of the crucial tasks of the executive to know when to say, "Enough is enough. Let's stop improving. There are too many patches on those pants."

Don't assume that there is just the one right strategy for innovations. Every one requires thinking through anew. Don't say, "We have been successful six times in introducing the new this way, so that must be the *right* way. That's our formula now." And if it doesn't work don't blame the "Stupid Public". Say instead, "Maybe this needs to be done differently." Before you go into an innovative strategy, don't say, "This is how we do it." Say, "let's find out what this needs. Where is the right place in the market? Who are the customers, the beneficiaries? What is the right way to deliver it? What is the right way to introduce it? Let's not start out with what we know. Let's start out with *what we need to learn.*"

When a strategy or an action doesn't seem to be working, the rule is, "If at first you don't succeed, try once more. Then do something else." The first time around, a new strategy very often doesn't work. Then one must sit down and ask what has been learned. "Maybe we pushed too hard when we had success. Or we thought we had won and slackened our efforts." Or maybe the service isn't quite right. Try to improve it, to change it and make another major effort. Maybe, though I am reluctant to encourage that, you should make a third effort. After that, go to work where the results are there is only so much time and so many resources, and there is so much work to be done.

There are exceptions. You can see some great achievements where people laboured in the wilderness for twenty-five years. But they are very rare. Most of the people who persist in the wilderness leave nothing behind but bleached bones. There are also true believers who are dedicated to a cause where success, failure, and results are irrelevant, and we need such people. They are our conscience. But very few of them achieve. Maybe their rewards are in Heaven. But that's not sure, either. "There is no joy in Heaven over empty churches", St. Augustine wrote sixteen hundred years ago to one of his monks who busily built churches all over the desert. So, if you have no results, try a second time. Then look at it carefully and move on to something else.

Job of a Leader

The most successful leader of this century was Winston Churchill. But for twelve years, from 1928 until Dunkirk in 1940, he was totally on the sidelines, almost discredited—because there was no need for a Churchill. Things were routine or, at any rate, looked routine. When the catastrophe came, thank goodness, he was available. Fortunately or unfortunately, the one predictable thing in any organisation is the crisis. That always comes. That's when you *do* depend on the leader.

The most important task of an organisation's leader is to anticipate crisis. Perhaps not to avert it, but to anticipate it. To wait until the crisis hits is already abdication. One has to make the organisation capable of anticipating the storm, weathering it, and in fact, being ahead of it. That is called innovation, constant renewal. You cannot prevent a major catastrophe, but you can build an organisation that is battle-ready, that has high morale, and also has been through a crisis, knows how to behave, trusts itself, and where people trust one another. In military training, the first rule is to instill soldiers with trust in their officers, because without trust they won't fight.

The Problems of Success

Problems of success have ruined more organisations than has failure, partly because if things go wrong, everybody knows they have to go to work. Success creates its own euphoria. You outrun your resources. And you retire on the job, which may be the most difficult thing to fight. I'm now in California instead of New York University, where I was for twenty years, in part because the Graduate Business School at NYU decided to cut back rather than grow with the growing student demand. That's why I left. When I started to build a management school at Claremont, I made sure that we did not overextend ourselves. I was very careful to ensure that we kept the faculty first rate but small, and that we used adjuncts, part-time people, then built a strong administration. And then we could run with success. If the market grows, you have to grow with it, or you become marginal.

I am arguing these days with our pastor, who wants to keep our church small. This is in a community where we have a lot of young people, students, and a lot of people in retirement homes who want to come to church. My very nice and able pastor likes to keep it small so that he knows everybody. I said to him, "Look, Father Michael, it won't work." Five years after he had come in, the church began to shrink. The lesson for the leaders of non-profits is that one has to grow with success. But one also has to make sure that one doesn't become unable to adjust. Sooner or later, growth slows down and the institution plateaus. Then it has to be able to maintain its momentum, its flexibility, its vitality, and its vision. Otherwise, it becomes frozen.

Hard Choices

Non-profit organisations have no "bottom line." They are prone to consider everything they do to be righteous and moral and to serve a cause, so they are not willing to say, if it doesn't produce results then maybe we should direct our resources elsewhere. Non-profit organisations need the discipline of organised abandonment perhaps even more than a business does. They need to face up to critical choices.

Some of these choices are very difficult. I have a friend, a Catholic priest, who is Vicar General of a large diocese. The bishop called him in to deal with the shortage of priests. Which services should they keep and which should they abandon? There is the terrible dilemma of Catholic schools in a big metropolitan archdiocese where 97 percent of the kids are not Catholics and aren't going to be Catholics; they're fleeing the misery of the public schools. I've been arguing with the diocese for years. Some of the priests say, "Our first task is to save souls; it's not to educate people. Let's put our few priests and nuns on our first priority." And I say, "Look, it says in the Bible, 'But the greatest of these is Charity', and that's what you are doing. You cannot possibly leave those kids in the lurch. That's a value choice, and it's critical that it's faced up to and not pushed under the rug, as we like to do."

Once you acknowledge that, you can then innovate—provided you organise yourself to look for innovation. Non-profit institutions need innovation as much as businesses or governments. And we know how to do it.

The starting point is to recognise that change is not a threat. It's an opportunity. We know where to look for changes. Here are a few examples:

Unexpected Success in Your Own Organisation

Some institutions of higher education, for instance, have learned that continuing education of already highly educated adults is not a luxury, or something to bring in additional money, or good public relations. It is becoming the central thrust of our knowledge society. So, they have organised themselves and their faculties to attract the doctors, engineers, and executives who want and need to go back to school.

Population Changes

About twelve years ago, the Girl Scouts of the U.S.A. realised that demographic shifts in the United States, with the fast growth of minorities, were creating a new frontier for the organisation—new needs and the opportunity to change. They now have a 15 percent enrollment of minority kids, which explains why they kept growing even though the total number of girls of scouting age fell quite steadily during that period.

Changes in Mind-Set and Mentality

Very few factors have so altered our view of society as the women's movement of the last twenty years. What opportunities does it create? As you will see a little later on in the interview with Father Leo Bartel in Part Four, it created the opportunity in one diocese to expand dramatically despite a sharp drop in the number of priests and sisters. Another example; about fifteen years ago, one of our largst volunteer organisations, the American Heart Association, realised that, even though its original big job—research—was not yet accomplished, a new opportunity had opened to take advantage of the tremendous growth in health awareness by the American public. It decided to redirect its national forces.

The lesson is, Don't wait. Organise yourself for systematic innovation. Build the search for opportunities, inside and outside, into your organisation. Look for changes as indications of an opportunity for innovation. To build all this into your system, you, as the leader of the organisation, have to set the example, How. can we set up systems to release energy that will allow the proper innovative decisions to be made and implemented and, at the same time, encourage the operation to go on at the necessary level while it is being changed? Let me try to outline a simple series of steps.

First, organise yourself to see the opportunity. If you don't look out the window, you won't see it. What makes this particularly important is that most of our current reporting systems don't reveal opportunities; they report problems. They report the past. Most answer questions we have already asked. So, we have to go beyond our reporting systems. And whenever you need a change, ask: If this were an opportunity for us, what would it be?

Then, to implement the innovation effectively, there are a few points you must be aware of. First, the most common mistake—the one that kills more innovations than anything else—is the attempt to build too much reinsurance into the change, to cover your flank, not to alienate yesterday. The Japanese made that mistake in the one area where their export drive failed significantly: telephones. They had the technology but tried to hedge their bets by selling switchboards that were both electromechanical (and therefore could be plugged into existing old systems) *and* electronic. The electronic switchboards force customers to tear out their old equipment, even though it may be perfectly good. But those who did go either into expansion or improvement of their existing system decided to pull out the old and go straight to the state-of-the-art.

The same sort of mistakes can be found in the pharmaceutical industry and in educational programs. Twenty years ago, a good many hospitals, seeing the trend toward taking care of patients outside the hospital, built outpatient clinics into the hospital. That didn't work. The free-standing surgical clinic, however, *did* work because it was not in the hospital.

Next, you have the problem of organising the new. It must be organised separately. Babies don't belong in the living room, they belong in the nursery. If you put new ideas into operating units—whether it's a theological seminary or an automobile plant—the solving of the daily crisis will always take precedence over introducing tomorrow. So, when you try to develop the new within an existing operation, you are always postponing tomorrow. It must be set up separately. And yet you have to make sure the existing operations don't lose the excitement of the new entirely. Otherwise, they become not only hostile but paralysed.

The Innovative Strategy

Next, you need an innovative strategy: a way to bring the new to the marketplace. Successful innovation finds a target of opportunity. Somebody who is receptive, who welcomes the new, who wants to succeed and, at the same time, has enough stature, enough clout in the organisation so that, if it works for him or her, the rest of the organisation will say, Well, there must be something to it.

I am always being asked, "If you were running a metropolitan museum, or a major public library, or a relief or service agency in a community, would you have part of your organisation set up some kind of small task force committed to R&D or to marketing? Some group working within the organisation that would be weighing the possibilities of innovation for the organisation?"

Well, the answer is yes and the answer is no. Yes, because you need a few people who do the work, who have the time to do it. It's hard work. No, because if you isolate the planning, you're going to end up overlocking perhaps the small but crucial things. Let me give you a very simple example. The executives of a big museum decided to move from the old-time museum, which kept the art works in and the people out, to the modern kind of museum, which is basically an educational community. They set up a separate planning group, which did a magnificent job planning exhibitions and publicity and so on. But being isolated from operations, the planners overlooked a few 'housekeeping' details. They forgot, for instance, that you need a much bigger parking lot. Also, if you suddenly have three hundred fourth graders in, you need toilets. When they opened, you cannot imagine the pandemonium. And that's typical.

If you first plan and then try to sell, you're going to miss the important things. But you also waste years of time. Selling has to be built into planning, and that means involving the operating people. But don't forget one thing: everything new requires hard work on the part of true believers—and true believers are *not* available part time.

The Churchills may be very rare. But another group is, fortunately, quite common. These are the people who can look at a situation and say: This is not what I was hired to do or what I expected to do, but this is what the job requires—and then roll up their sleeves and go to works. I know a college president who was conned into taking his job with the usual promises by the board that it would raise the money. He came out of tax-supported state universities. He arrived with a wonderful program of faculty recruitment and educational reform, took one good look, and came to me, very unhappy. Somebody has to raise money, he said, otherwise that institution won't be there in five or ten years. And I said, You know there is only one person who can raise money in a college—the president. And he said, I'm afraid you're right. He found an exceedingly able man on his faculty who for five years ran the school, while the president concentrated on raising money, in which he proved himself incredibly able. He saved that institution.

Let me give you another example of a rural electric cooperative, one of the large ones, founded during the 1930s when the American farmer couldn't get any power. Well, by now everybody has power, so the question is: What do we do now? There was strong sentiment on the board and in the membership for selling out to the nearest large power company. A new chief executive came in, took a look, and said: "Yes, as an electric cooperative we have fulfilled our mission, but as a community development organisation, it has only begun. Here is a tremendous farm crisis [this was in the early eighties]. All kinds of basic social services need to be supplied to our farm members, and they can only be supplied by somebody with a distribution system."

He made all the difference. Farm prices are still low and depressed, but this six-county system is one of the few farm areas we have that is, I wouldn't say prosperous, but doing well because of the action this man took seeing the opportunity. And it's not that uncommon. *This* is effective crisis leadership.

How to Pick a Leader

If I were on a selection committee to choose a leader for a non-profit organisation and there were a roster of men and women as candidates, what would I look for? First, I would look at what the individuals have done, what their strengths are. Most selection committees I know are overly concerned with how *poor* the candidate is. Most of the questions I get are not: What is he or she good at, but we think this person is not too good at dealing with students, or what have you. The first thing to look for is strength—you can only perform with strength—and what they have done with it.

Second, I would look at the institution and ask: What is the one immediate key challenge. It may be raising money. It may be rebuilding the morale of the organisation. It may be redefining its mission. It may be bringing in new technology. If I looked today for an administrator of a large hospital, I might look for the ability to convert the hospital from a provider of sickness care to a manager of sickness-care providers, because more and more will be done outside the hospital. I would try to match the strengths with the needs.

Then I would look for—call it character or integrity. A leader sets an example, especially a strong leader. He or she is somebody on whom people, especially younger people, in the organisation model themselves. Many years ago I learned from a very wise old man, who was head of a large, worldwide organisation. I was about twenty, not even that—and he was in his late seventies, famous for putting the right people into the right enterprises all over the globe. I asked him: "What do you look for?" And he said: "I always ask myself, would I want one of my sons to work under that person? If he is successful, then young people will imitate him. Would I want my son to look like this?" This, I think, is the ultimate question.

I've seen lots of businesses and all of us have seen lots of governments survive with mediocre leaders for quite a long time. In the non-profit agency, mediocrity in leadership shows up almost immediately. One difference clearly is that the non-profit has a number of bottom lines—not just one. In business, you can debate whether profit is really an adequate measuring stick; it may not be over the short term, but it is the ultimate one over the long term. In government, in the last analysis, you've got to get reelected. But in non-profit management, there is no such one determinant. You deal with balance, synthesis, a combination of bottom lines for performance.

Certainly, the non-profit executive does not have the luxury of dealing with one dominant constituency, either. In a publicly listed company, the shareholder is the ultimate constituent. In government, it is the voter. When you look at the school board, a public service agency, or a church, however, you have a multiplicity of constituencies—each of which can say no and none of which can say yes. The multiplicity of constituencies is reflected in your boards, your trustees, who are likely to be intensely involved in running the agency. You could say public schools are governmental, but the school board is not governmental. It has the constituency role. That's what causes all the difficulty for school superintendents. They are really public service agencies rather than government agencies.

You can't be satisfied in non-profit organisations with doing adequately as a leader. You have to do exceptionally well, because your agency is committed to a cause. You want people as leaders who take a great view of the agency's functions, people who take their roles seriously—not *themselves* seriously. Anybody in that leadership position who thinks he is a great man or a woman will kill himself—and the agency.

Your Personal Leadership Role

The new leader of a non-profit doesn't have much time to establish himself or herself. Maybe a year. To be effective in that short a time, the role the leader takes has to fit in terms of the mission of the institution and its values. All of us play roles—as parents, as teachers, and as leaders. To work, the role has to fit in three dimentions. First, the role has to fit you—who you are. No comic actor has ever been able to play Hamlet. The role you take also has to fit the task. And, finally, the role has to fit expectations.

One of the more brilliant young men I ever hired as a teacher completely failed in the college classroom. In teaching freshmen, he abdicated his authority, and the kids revolted. He didn't understand that nineteen-year-old freshmen in an undergraduate college expect a teacher to have authority.

You have two things to build on: the quality of the people in the organisation, and the new demands you make on them. What these new demands will be can be determined by analysis, or by perception, or by a combination of both. That depends on how you operate. I am a perceptual person. I look. But I've also seen very able and effective people who are totally paper-oriented. They take a sharp pencil and come out right.

There are simply no such things as "leadership traits" or "leadership characteristics." Of course, some people are better leaders than others. By and large, though, we are talking about skills that perhaps cannot be tought but they can be learned by most of us. True, some people ganuinely cannot learn the skills. they may not be important to them; or they'd rather be followers. But most of us can learn them.

The leaders who work most effectively, it seems to me, never say "I." And that's not because they hae trained themselves not to say "I." They don't *think* "I." They think "we"; they think "team." They understand their job to be to make the team function. They accept the responsibility and don't sidestep it, but "We" gets the credit. There is an identification (very often, quite unconscious) with the task and with the group. This is what creates trust, what enables you to get the task done.

In Shakeseare's *Henry V*, the young prince whose father just died—he is now king—rides out. Falstaff, the old disreputable knight who has been the prince's boon companion in drinking and wenching, calls up to his "Sweet Prince Hal", and the new king rides by without even a look at him. Falstaff is cruelly hurt. He raised the prince because the old king was a very poor father and a cold one, and the young man found warmth only with that disreputable drunkard. Yet Henry is now king and has to set different standards for himself because he is visible. As a leader, you are visible; incredibly visible. And you have expectations to fulfill.

Then there is the story of the one leading German statesman before World War I who saw the catastrophe Europe was sliding into and tried desperately to reverse the trend. He was the ambassador to London in the early days of the century—a leading dove. But he resigned his ambassadorship because the new English King, Edward VII, was a notorious womaniser who liked the diplomatic corps to give him stag parties at which the most popular London courtesans would pop naked out of cakes. The ambassador said he was not willing to be a pimp when he saw himself in a mirror shaving in the morning. I don't think he could have averted World War I. Still, politically, he may have made the wrong decision. And yet, I think, it was the essence of leadership. You are visible; you'd better realise that you are constantly on trial. The rule is: I don't want to see a pimp in the mirror when I shave in the morning. If you do see one, then your people will see one, too.

"To every leader there is a season." There is profoundity in that statement, but it's not quite that simple. Winston Churchill in ordinary, peaceful, normal times would not have been very effective. He needed the challenge. Probably the same is true of Franklin. D. Roosevelt, who was basically a lazy man. I don't think that FDR would have been a good president in the 1920s. His adrenalin wouldn't have produced. On the other hand, there are people who are very good when things are pretty routine, but who can't take the stress of an emergency. Most organisations need somebody who can lead regardless of the weather. What matters is that he or she works on the basic competences.

As the first such basic competence, I would put the willingness, ability, and self-discipline to listen. Listening is not a skill; it's a discipline. Anybody can do it. All you have to do is keep your mouth shut. The second essential competence is the willingness to communicate, to make yourself understood. That requires infinite patience. We never outgrow age three in that respect. You have to tell us again and again and again. And demonstrate what you mean. The next important competence is not to alibi yourself. Say: "This doesn't work as well as it should. Let's take it back and re-engineer it." We either do things to perfection, or we don't do them. We don't do things to get by. Working that way creates pride in the organisation.

The last basic competence is the willingness to realise how unimportant you are compared to the task. Leaders need objectivity, a certain detachment. They subordinate themselves to the task, but don't identify themselves with the task. The task remains both bigger than they are, and different. The worst thing you can say about a leader is that on the day he or she left, the organisation collapsed. When that happens, it means the so-called leader had sucked the place dry. He or she hasn't built. They may have been effective operators, but they have not created vision. Louis XIV was supposed to have said, *"L'etat, c'est moil !"* (The state, that's me!). He died in the early eighteenth century and the long, not-so-slow slide into the French Revolution immediately began.

When effective non-profit leaders have the capacity to maintain their personality and individuality, even though they are totally dedicated, the task will go on after them. They also have a human existence outside the task. Otherwise they do things for personal aggrandisement, in the belief that this furthers the cause. They become self-centered and vain. And above all, they become jealous. One of the great strengths of Churchill and one of the great weaknesses of FDR was that Churchill, to the very end, when he was in his nineties, pushed and furthered young politicians. That is a hallmark of the truly effective leader, who doesn't feel threatened by strength. In his last years, FDR systematically cut down everybody who showed any signs of independence.

I would not want any person to give his or her life to an organisation. One gives one's very best efforts. What attracts people to an organisation are high standards, because high standards create self-respect and pride. Most of us want to contribute. When you look at schools where kids learn and schools where kids don't, it's not the quality of the teaching that's different. The school in which kids learn expects them to learn. Many years ago, I did a survey of Boy Scout Councils with tremendous differences in performance. In the performing ones, they expected the volunteers, the scoutmasters, and so n, to put in very hard work. And I mean hard work, not just appearing Friday night for a couple of hours. The ones with high demands attracted the volunteers and attracted and kept the boys. So it is the job of the leaders to set high standards on one condition—that they be performance-focused.

Most leaders I've seen were neither born nor made. They were self-made. We need far too many leaders to depend only on the naturals. The best example of one who surely was not born a leader, had no training, and made himself into a very effective one, was Harry Truman. When Truman became president, he was totally unprepared. An ordinary politician, he was chosen as vice president because he presented no threat to FDR. Truman not only said, "I am president now and the buck stops here", but he also asked, "What are the key tasks?" His entire preparation had been in domestic affairs. He forced himself to accept the fact that the key tasks for his administration were outside the United States and not the New Deal (much to the disappointment of the New Deal liberals, beginning with Mrs. Roosevelt). He forced himself to take a cram course in foreign affairs and to focus—painfully—on what he considered to be key tasks.

In a way, the hospital as we know it today is the creation of a totally obscure and forgotten Catholic hospital administrator of the 1930s and 1940s (who taught me all I know), Sister Justina in Evanston, Indiana. She was the first person to think through what patient care is. For her contributions she got very few thanks in her life, especially not from the physicians, but she was a born leader. She was retiring, shy, understated, very conscious of the fact that her formal education had stopped in first grade in an Irish country school. But there was a job to be done. And that, again and again, is what really makes the leaders. They are self-made.

Douglas MacArthur was a brilliant man and probably the last great strategist, but that wasn't his great strength. He built a team second to none because he put the task first. He was also unbelievably vain, with a tremendous contempt for humanity, because he was certain that no one came close to him in intelligence. Nevertheless, he forced himself in every single staff conference to start the presentation with the most junior officer. He did not allow anybody to interrupt. This contributed incredibly to his ability to build an organisation that was willing to fight against the vastly superior enemy and win. It is very clear from his letters that this didn't come easily to him, never. He always had to force himself. It wasn't his nature, but it *was* the key task, and so it had to be done.

Tom Watson, Sr., the creator of IBM, began as a self-centered, imperious man – vain, with a very short fuse. He forced himself to build a team, a winning team. He once let somebody go who I thought was very able and I asked why. Watson told me: "He is not willing to educate me. I am not a technical man, I am a salesman. But this is a technical company, and if they don't educate me in technology, I can't give them the leadership they need." It's that willingness to make yourself competent in the task that's needed that creates leaders.

When Ted Houser took over in the early 1950s, Sears, Roebuck had twenty-five years of unbroken success. Houser had been a buying strategist and a statistician, purely a figures man. He looked at the company and asked: What does it need so that it can be successful *another* twenty-five years? He concluded that it needed managers. So he forced himself into taking the leadership of Sear's manager development in a very effective and yet very quiet way. Everybody down to the manager of the smallest store knew that the chairman in Chicago was watching him, and would know whether he was developing people. Sears hasn't had a new idea since 1950, yet it remained very successful for twenty-five or thirty years, almost up to 1980, because it had the people. That's what Ted Houser built.

The Balance Decision

One of the key tasks of the leader is to balance up the long range and the short range, the big picture and the pesky little details. You are always paddling a canoe with two outriggers—balancing—while managing a non-profit. One is the balance between seeing only the big picture and forgetting the individual person who sits there—one lonely young man in need of help. I've heard of hospitals that talk health-care statistics and forget the mother with a crying baby in the emergency room. That kind of failing is fairly easy to correct. Being on the firing line a few days, a few weeks, a year, usually does it. The opposite danger is becoming the prisoner of operations. That's much harder to avoid. The effective people do it very largely through their work in assiciations and other organisations. The successful chief executive of one of our major community service organisations, one of the very large Scout Councils, sits on three boards of which only one is a community service organisation—quite intentionally. And she also sits on an advisory committee of the city government, That way she is forced to see the same issues she faces in her own organisation through the other end of the telescope. That works.

I've also seen it done on a smaller, much smaller, scale. A dean I worked with for many years, whom I considered singularly successful, went on the American Council of Deans. I said to him, "Paul, you are so busy, why do you do it?" And he said, "I'm too close to the details. Once a month, I need to see what the overall issues really are." That, too, is a fairly effective way.

Let me say there are always balancing problems in managing non-profits. This is only one example. Another, which I think is even harder to handle, is the balance between concentrating resources on one goal and enough diversification. If you concentrate, you will get maximum results. But it's also very risky. Not only may you have chosen the wrong concentration, but—in military terms—you leave your flanks totally uncovered. And there's not enough playfulness; it doesn't stir the imagination. You need that, so that there will be diversity, especially as any single task eventually becomes obsolete. But diversity can easily degenerate into splintering.

The even more critical balance, and the toughest to handle, is between being too cautious and being rash. Finally, there is timing—and this is always of the essence. You know the people who always expect results too soon and pull up the radishes to see whether they've set root, and the ones who never pull up the radishes because they're sure they're never ripe enough. Those are, in philosophical terms, Aristotelian Prudences, so to speak. How to find the right Mean.

It's actually fairly easy to deal with people who want results too soon. I'm one of them. And I've taught myself that if I expect something to happen in three months, I say, make it five. But I've also seen people who say three years when they should say three months. That's very hard to counteract. As in all Aristotelian means, the first law is "know thyself." Know what is your degenerative tendency.

I've seen more institutions damaged by too much caution than by rashness, though I've seen both. Maybe I'm conscious of it because I was over-cautious when I ran institutions, or was part of the running. I did not take risks, especially financial risks, I should have taken. On the other hand, I've seen one of the country's universities almost ruined—Pittsburgh, in the 1950s—by a brilliant man who came in and tried to convert what was a fair metropolitan university into a world-class research institution in three years. He thought money would do it. Instead, he almost killed the university, and it has never quite recovered. I've seen the same thing in a museum and the same thing in a symphony orchestra. So, one has to have balance, and again the only advice I can give is to make sure you know your degenerative tendency and try to counteract it.

Then there is the balance decision between opportunity and risk. One asks first: is the decision reversible? If it is, one usually can take even considerable risks. In the non-profit institution, you constantly must gauge whether the financial dimension of a risk is too great. That's all I can say. One looks at the decision: Is it reversible? And what kind of risk is it? Then one asks: Is it a risk we can afford? All right, if it goes wrong, it hurts a little. Or is it a risk that, if things go wrong, will kill us? Or the trickiest of them all, the risk we can't afford not to take. I've been in a similar situation recently. I sit on a museum board—and a big collection was offered to us, way beyond our means. I said, Damn the torpedoes, let's buy it. It's the last chance we have. It'll make us a world-class museum. We'll get the money somehow. The balance decisions are what we need non-profit leaders for, whether they are paid or volunteer.

The Don't's of Leadership

Finally, there are a few major don't's for leaders. Far too many leaders believe that what they do and why they do it must be obvious to everyone in the organisation. It never is. Far too many believe that when they announce things, everyone understands. No one does, as a rule. Yet very often one can't bring in people before the decision; there just isn't enough time for discussion or participation. Effective leaders have to spend a little time on making themselves understood. They sit down with their people and say: This is what we were faced with. These are the alternatives we saw, the alternatives we considered. They asks what is your opinion? Otherwise the organisation will say: Don't these dummies at the top know anything? What's going on here? Why haven't they considered this or that? But if you can say, Yes, we considered it, but still reached this decision, people will understand and will go along. They may say we wouldn't have decided that way, but at least upstairs, they just didn't shoot from the hip.

And the second don't. Don't be afraid of strengths in your organisation. This is the besetting sin of people who run organisations. Of course, able people are ambitious. But you run far less risk of having able people around who want to push you out than you risk by being served by mediocrity. And finally, don't pick your successor alone. We tend to pick people who remind us of ourselves when we were twenty years younger. First, this is pure delusion. Second, you end up with carbon copies, and carbon copies are weak. The old rule both in military organisations and in the Catholic Church is that leaders don't pick their own successors. They're consulted, but they don't make the decision. I've seen many cases in business—but even more in non-profit institutions—where able people picked a good number two to succeed them. Somebody who is very able—

provided you tell him or her what to do. It doesn't work. Partly out of emotional commitment, partly out of habit the perfect number two is put into the top spot, and the whole organisation suffers. The last time I saw this was in one of the world's largest community chests. Fortunately the number two who was picked by his predecessor because he was so much like her realised after a year that he didn't belong in the top job and was utterly miserable in it—and he left before either he or the organisation had been badly damaged. But that is a rare exception. The last don't's are: Don't hog the credit, and Don't knock your subordinates. One of the very ablest men I've seen do this headed one of the most challenging new tasks in a non-profit organisation I know. His alumni now work for everybody else but for his organisation because the moment they went to work for him, he saw nothing but their weaknesses. He didn't promote any of his people and never sang their praises. A leader has responsibility to his subordinates, to his associates.

Those are the don't's.

The most important do, I have said again and again already: Keep your eye on the task, not on yourself. The task matters, and you are a servant.

What the Leader Owes

PETER DRUCKER: Max, you have the reputation in your common but also in the institutions which you serve as a board member is being the leader in developing people. Is there any one thing you would stress about that?

MAX DE PREE: I would have to begin with a very personal observation, which is that I believe, first of all, that each of us is mad in the image of God. That we come to life with a tremendous diversity of gifts. I think from there, a leader needs to see himself in a position of indebtedness. Leaders are given the gift of leadership by those who choose or agree to follow. We're basically volunteer nation. I think this means that people choose a leader to a great extent on the basis of what they believe that leader can contribute to the person's ability to achieve his or her goals in life. This puts the leader in the position of being indebted—in the sense of what he or she owes to the organisation.

One relatively straightforward way of looking at it is that the leader owes certain assets to an organisation. In some organisations, that would be the ability to recruit the right people. Another important asset is the ability to raise the necessary funds. Another area isn't quite as clear, and I would put that under the general heading of a legacy: the values of the organisation. The leader may not be the author of those values, but the leader is accountable for expressing them, making them clear, and ensuring to the people in the organisation that the values will be lived up to in a way in which decisions are made. Vision comes under the heading of legacy. Agreed-upon work processes come under this heading. If leaders say, "If you come to work in this organisation, I can promise you that we're going to have a participatory process", they are indebted to provide that. An element that is clearly, to me at least, common ground—whether one is in the profit-making or non-profit organisation—is that this whole matter of people development needs to be oriented primarily toward the *person*, and not primarily toward the organisation.

PETER DRUCKER: You develop people, not jobs, is what you are saying.

MAX DE PREE: Yes, and I'm saying too that when you take the risk of developing people, the odds are very good that the organisation will get what it needs.

PETER DRUCKER: But you are also implying, I take it, that you can only develop what the person has. Not what the person ain't got?

MAX DE PREE: That's right. We're talking about building on what people are—not about changing them. To understand their gifts, to understand what their potential is. We tend, in organisations, to put a lot of emphasis on the achievement of goals, but when we're talking about the development of a person, we have a much higher aim. Here we're talking about potential.

That attitude about people development, I believe, also applies, by the way, to the development of an organisation. I think if we focus on goal achievement, we miss the chance we have of realising our potential. Goal achievement is an annual matter related to the annual plan. But the realisation of our potential, that's a life matter.

PETER DRUCKER: Don't you really look at two aspects? You look at the gifts of people, their potential, their strength, what they could be if only they used a little better what they have. But you also look at the objective needs, the objective requirements, the opportunities for accomplishment. Don't you always look inside and out?

MAX DE PREE: You need to make a connection between this matter of realising potential and doing it in a very real environment. One needs to be accountable, and the accountability needs to be connected to the needs of the organisations.

PETER DRUCKER: And don't you also need achievement to grow?

MAX DE PREE: You do need achievement, and I also happen to feel that that's one of the things for which the leader is partially accountable. I believe the leader needs to assign opportunities and assign work that can be realised. I don't think leaders ought to assign work that's impossible.

PETER DRUCKER: For this person?

MAX DE PREE: For this person, that's right.

PETER DRUCKER: So the leader starts out with what this person really is good at, and then tries to place the person where the strength can redound to performance?

MAX DE PREE: Yes, and, of course, any time we talk about accountability and about achievement, it has to be clear that we are going to delegate thoroughly. Delegate with a certain abandon so that people have space in which to realise potential, in which to be accountable, in which to achieve. I don't believe we can achieve organisational goals without that congruency. I believe it is more the responsibility of the leader to forge that integration than it is of the individual. It's the kind of thing that a follower has a right to expect from a leader.

PETER DRUCKER: You implied a little earlier, Max, that the first duty of a leader was to have followers. In fact, the definition of a leader, the only definition, is somebody who has followers. What is necessary for this? A clear mission? A clear vision?

MAX DE PREE: A leader must have vision. It is natural for a leader to be a person who is primarily future-oriented. I don't mean that to be a duplication of having vision. Those are not exactly the same things. To talk more specifically about the duties of a leader, I happen to believe that the first duty of a leader is to define reality. Every organisation, in order to be healthy, to have renewal processes, to survive, has to be in touch with reality.

PETER DRUCKER: How would you define reality for a liberal arts college with its 2,500 students?

MAX DE PREE: One reality, for instance, might be that it happens to be a tuition-driven college. If you don't understand that clearly, you will not put the right amount of emphasis on the recruitment of students. So it's important that the leader sees and defines clearly for the group what reality is.

PETER DRUCKER: A little earlier you said something very important which, in my opinion, very few people in the non-profit institutions yet realise. Most of us still operate on the assumption that people have no choice. They have to take a job. This was true a hundred years ago. But today there are fifty different ways we can earn a living. You call it electiveness, Max, I believe. We have to deserve the person who works for us. We owe him or her, which is what you meant by indebtedness. Because they are not committed to us by necessity; they are committed to us by choice.

MAX DE PREE: People have a lot of choice in where they're going to work, what kind of work they're going to do. They have a lot of choice about mid-career changes. We're only about a generation away from people who, once they had chosen a career, had to stick with it. That's all different today.

PETER DRUCKER: That has to be built into the development processes, I suspect.

MAX DE PREE: Yes. And I think it is related to the kinds of promises that the leader gives. At the heart of that is the whole matter of opportunity. Opportunity is clearly one of the most important things that we seek today in our working lives.

PETER DRUCKER: Opportunity for what?

MAX DE PREE: For self-realisation, for being part of a social body that is attractive and rewarding. Opportunity for doing work which will help me to reach my potential. Opportunity to be involved with something that's meaningful. Opportunity to be an integral part of something. We do not develop vital surviving organisations unless we take into account these needs for meaningful work, for a chance at reaching our potential for good social relationships.

PETER DRUCKER: Instead of bemoaning that young people are lazy or self-centered, I think one says: what do they have? They hae a tremendous desire to contribute. Maybe they want to succeed too fast. But how do we use what they have to make them want to belong? What is it that the non-profit institution can do to that newcomer, that young person, to acquire self-discipline?

MAX DE PREE: That's a very difficult question. I think it's better to erron the side of being more demanding of a person than of being less demanding.

PETER DRUCKER: And be willing to have a high casualty rate?

MAX DE PREE: Yes. But organisationally speaking, the casualty isn't always necessarily terminal. One of the things that I feel we need to understand better in organisation life is the role of grace. Mistakes are not terminal. Mistakes are part of education with, of course, some exceptions. When we challenge people on the high side, the odds are much better that we're going to get *both* better performance and more development of the person.

PETER DRUCKER: On two conditions, I would say, Max. One has to be willing to give the person who tries a second and perhaps even third chance, but I wouldn't waste my breath on people who don't try. And then there has to be a mentor if you give that much load, that much demand, that much responsibility to beginners—and I'm all for it. I would never have learned anything if I hadn't been loaded to the gunnels by my first two bosses; they were totally unpermissive and demanding. And they did not hesitate to chastise me. But they were willing to listen to me. They were sparing with praise, but always willing to encourage. I couldn't even guess how much I owe them. I think one needs an enormous amount of responsibility, especially as a beginner, but one also does need a mentor. How do you provide that?

MAX DE PREE: In my experience, it's never been easy formally to establish mentorship programs. I think that mentorship, in a certain sense, depends on chemistry. People make a connection. One person feels ready to help another. One person feels ready to accept help from a certain person. I believe that the best way to have mentorship take place is to reward it visibly when it happens rather than to try to structure it.

PETER DRUCKER: Look out for those people—and they're not usually very conspicuous—who do a job developing people, and recognise them, praise them, feature them.

MAX DE PREE: That's right.

PETER DRUCKER: Consider it one of the key functions in the organisation?

MAX DE PREE: Yes. And the leader better make sure that those people know how the leader personally feels about their contribution to the organisation. That cannot slip by unnoticed.

PETER DRUCKER: Max, you have been talking about "the" leader, and yet you have been famous in your own organisation for building a strong team of colleagues and conspicuous in the organisations where you were on the board for stressing the team again and again. So, what are the ways of building a team? Especially in organisations in which you have professionals on the staff and volunteers and an elected board, and so on, held together by a common mission and common vision.

MAX DE PREE: I think the first element is to understand the task. What is the job that has to be done?

PETER DRUCKER: The key activities?

MAX DE PREE: The key activities of the team. The second one is selecting people, and that's a high-risk process. When we select people, I think we have to understand that we're going to make some adjustments in assignments. Then we assign the work very clearly with a lot of interaction. We agree on what the process is going to be for getting that work done. We agree on timetables where those are appropriate. We agree on how we're going to measure performance. That all sounds fairly conventional, but it's hard work.

There's one further element: the way in which you judge the quality of leadership by what I would call the tone of the body, not by the charisma of the leader, not by how much publicity the company gets, or the leader gets, or any of that stuff. How well does the body adjust to change? How well does the body deal with conflict? How well does the body meet the needs of the constituency or customers, whatever it is? That, in the end, is the way you judge the quality of leadership.

PETER DRUCKER: Would you include in your tone of the body also what happens when that leader passes off the scene?

MAX DE PREE: Suecessior is one of the key responsibilities of leadership.

PETER DRUCKER: Let me try to wrap up this interview and pull it together.

We are all used to talking about the leader as the servant of the organisation. And you, Max, stressed that, but you stressed something we are not hearing very often, when you talked about the indebtedness of the leader: that the leader starts out with the realisation that he and the organisation owe; they owe the customers, the clients, the constituency, whether they are parishioners, or patients, or students. They owe the followers, whether that's faculty, or employees, or volunteers. And what they owe really to enable people to realise their potential, to realise their purpose in serving the organisation.

Summary: The Action Implications

We hear a great deal these days about leadership, and it's high time we did. But, actually, mission comes first. Non-profit institutions exist for the sake of their mission. They exist to make a difference in society and in the life of the individual. They exist for the sake of their mission, and this must never be forgotten. The first task of the leader is to make sure that everybody sees the mission, hears it, lives it. If you lose sight of your mission, you begin to stumble and it shows very; very fast. And yet, mission needs to be thoughts through, needs to be changed.

The basic rationale for the organisation may be there for a very long time. As long as the human race is around, we'll be miserable sinners. And as long as the human race is around, we will have sick people who need to be taken care of. We know that no matter how well a society does, there will be alcoholics, there will be people in trouble with drugs, there will be people who need the Salvation Army to bring compassion to them and a little help, and an attempt to rehabilitate them, and children will have to learn and go to school. Boys and girls, as they grow up, will need scouting and experiences that form their character, that give them a role model, that give them direction and employ them intelligently so that they learn something.

We will have to look at the mission again and again to think through whether it needs to be refocused because demographics change, because we should abandon something that produces no result and eats up resources, because we have accomplished an objective. A good example is the school that is largely in crisis because it has achieved its original objective of getting every kind of child to go to school and stay there for years, and now we have to think through what we really do expect of the school. And this will be, in many ways, quite different from what the schoolmasters through the ages were striving for when nine out of ten kids never had the opportunity of organised schooling. Therefore, it is vitally important to start out from the outside. The organisation that starts out from the inside and then tries to find places to put its resources is going to fritter itself away. Above all, it's going to focus on yesterday. One looks to the outside for opportunity, for a need.

At the same time, the mission is always long-range. It needs short-range efforts and very often short-range results. And yet it starts out with a long-range objective. There is a wonderful sentence in one of the sermons of that great poet and religious philosopher of the seventeenth century, John Donne: "Never start with tomorrow to reach eternity. Eternity is not being reached by small steps." So we start always with the long range, and then we feed back and say, What do we do *today?*

"Do" is the critical word. And that's the difference between what so often passes for planning in American business and what the Japanese do. It's not that they are better planners. It is that they start out by saying, Where should we be ten years hence? And we start by saying, What should be the bottom line for the quarter—which contrary to what most people in the United States believe, is higher in Japan than it is in American business, precisely because they start with the long range and feed back. As did all the companies in this country that have succeeded in staying viable, producing results for long the term. We have had some amazingly successful long-term companies—the Bell Telephone System, for fifty or sixty years; Sears, Roebuck for sixty years; General Motors, until recently. They all started out with a very clear long-range concept. Sears said: Our business is to be the informed and responsible buyer for the American family. And then one feeds back, and that may lead to very short-term moves—to Sears going into diamonds, for instance, right after World War II when the GIs came back and got married. But one always starts out with the long term. This is particularly important for non-profit institutions, precisely because they do not have an immediate bottom line, but also because they are there to serve.

But action is always short term. So one always has to ask: Is this action step leading us toward our basic long-range goal, or is it going to sidetrack us, going to divert us, going to make us lose sight of what we are here to do? This is the first question.

But also we need to be result-driven. We need to ask, Do we get adequate results for our efforts? Is this their best allocation? Yes, need is always a reason, but by itself it is not enough. There also have to be results. There also has to be something to point at and say, We have not worked in vain. So we are always looking at programs and projects with the question, Do they produce the right results? The leader's job is to make sure the right results are being achieved, the right things are being done.

One has the responsibility of allocate resources, particularly of course in organisations that depend heavily on volunteers, and heavily on donors. Leadership is accountable for results. And leadership always asks, Are we really faithful stewards of the talents entrusted to us? The talents, the gifts of people—the talents, the gifts of money. Leadership is *doing*. It isn't just thinking great thoughts; it isn't just charisma; it isn't play-acting. It is doing. And the first imperative of doing is to revise the mission, to refocus it, and to build and organise, and then abandon. It is asking ourselves whether, knowing what we now know, we would go into this again. Would we stress it? Would we pour more resources in, or would we taper off? That is the first action command for any mission.

It is also the one way of keeping an organisation lean and hungry and capable of doing new things. An old medical proverb says that the body can only take in the new if it eliminates the waste products. This is therefore the first action requirement: the constant resharpening, the constant refocusing, never really being satisfied. And the time to do this is when you are successful. If you wait until things have already started to go down, then it's very difficult. It is not impossible to turn around a declining institution, but an ounce of prevention is very much better than a ton of cure in the turnaround situation.

The next thing to do is to think through priorities. That's easy to say. But to act on it is hard because it always involves abandoning things that look very attractive, that people both inside and outside the organisation are pushing for. But if you don't concentrate your institution's resources, you are not going to get results. This may be the ultimate test of leadership: the ability to think through the priority decision and to make it stick.

Leadership is also example. The leader is visible; he stands for the organisation. He may be totally anonymous the moment he leaves that office and steps into his car to drive home. But inside the organisation, he or she is very visible, and this isn't just true of the small and local one, it is just as true of the big, national, or worldwide one. Leaders set examples. The leaders have to live up to the expectations regarding their behaviour. No matter that the rest of the organisation doesn't do it; the leader represents not only what we are, but, above all, what we know we should be.

So it is a very good rule when you do anything as a leader, to ask yourself, Is that what I want to see tomorrow morning when I look into the mirror? Is that the kind of person I want to see as my leader? And if you follow that rule, you will avoid the mistakes that again and again destroy leaders: sexual looseness in an organisation that preaches sexual rectitude, petty cheating, all the stupid things we do. Maybe the individual does them; well, that's his or her business. But a leader is not a private person; a leader represents. And then ask yourself, as a leader, what do I do to set standards in the organisation. What do I do to enable the organisation to tackle new challenges, to seize new opportunities, to innovate? What do I do? Not what does the organisation do? Take action responsibility. What are my own first priorities, and what are the organisation's first priorities, what *should* they be? These are the things that must be done.

You may think, that's fine for the CEO, but I'm only a volunteer putting in three hours a week, being a den mother or arranging flowers at a patient's bedside. *You are a leader.* The exciting thing, the new thing, is that we are creating a society of citizens in the old sense of people who actively work, rather than just passively vote and pay taxes. We are not doing it in business. There is a lot of talk of participative management; but there is not much reality to it, and in many ways, there never will be. The pressures are perhaps too great. In a country like ours, with almost 250 million people, even a small town has 50,000 inhabitants, and there is not very much a citizen can actually *do.* We could not, even in the smallest town, meaningfully revive the New England town meeting of two hundred years ago, when that New England town had one hundred twenty people or so.

But we are doing exactly this in the non-profit, the service institution, where increasingly there are only leaders. These are people who are paid and people who are not paid. In a church there are a very small number of people who are ordained, but one thousand people who work and do major tasks for the church who are not ordained, never will be, never get a penny. In the Girl Scouts of the U.S.A., there are one hundred volunteers for ever paid staff member, and each is doing a responsible task. We are creating tomorrow's society of citizens through the non-profit service institution. And in that society, everybody is a leader, every body is responsible, everybody acts. Everybody focuses himself of herself. Everybody raises the vision, the competence, and the performance of his or her organisation. Therefore, mission and leadership are not just things to read about, to listen to. They are things to do something about. Things that you can, and should, conver from good intentions and from knowledge into effective action, my next year, but tomorrow morning.

4

Professional Career Development

The provision of career growth and development is simultaneously an important reward for most high-technology and professional workers and one of the biggest sources of conflict for them. The nature of technical and professional work is such that continuing technical education and career development is essential. There also seem to be few role models for career engineers (Bailyn 1982) this lack exacerbates the potential for conflict for those professionals.

The key dilemma for technical and professional workers is whether to follow one's technical bent into isolation, with little chance of recognition, or to aspire to management, however untalented for it. Technical specialists will probably find it difficult to get the psychic income they need from managerial roles (Miller 1986; Bailyn 1982; Drucker 1988). That career route is not only more typical, but has much more cachet in this society.

There is an abundance of writing in the late 1980s about careers, by researchers and practitioners alike. Much of the attention is on the managerial career because it proceeds through various stages analoguous to life stages. Comparatively little attention is paid to technical careers, despite the projections of acute shortages in technical and professional expertise in the years ahead. Two of the few studies that do exist on career professionals within high-tech industries reveal that engineers still working as engineers had much more negative the reactions to their work than did other engineers who had moved into management (Bailyn 1982; Bailyn and Lynch 1983). Career engineers were less satisfied with their work and tended to see themselves as less successful, despite the fact that many of them were prised by their employing organisations. But those with managerial assignment are valued more highly than those without such assignments. Having a successful career in engineering usually means leaving it. Hughes (1958) said it best, thirty years ago: "The engineer who, at forty, can still use a slide rule of logarithmic table, and make a true drawing, is a failure" (p. 137).

Of course, there have been many attempts to offer parallel opportunities to professionals who choose to stay in their technical specialty rather than take managerial posts. But generally, these dual ladders have met with failure. Technical professionals have largely rejected them as well, in part because the reward structures are heavily biased toward management positions and titles (Drucker 1988). Given historical and current organisational realities, career development for technical professionals appears to be a contradiction in terms. That is, the type of work that challenges the technical professional is not consistent with the organisationally defined "successful" career path for these employees (Bailyn 1982). Thus, the dilemma as well as the challenge to management rests in resolving this contradiction.

Constraints on the High-Tech firm that Affect Accommodation

Environmental Context

Adjusting to changes in competitive environments characterised by explosive growth, rapid technological change, and problems with employment practices, economic downturns, and reduced federal support for research, requires that firms be able to adapt their strategy quickly to be effective in their markets. They are frequently called upon to make adjustments in procedures, in work relationships among professionals, and in their organisational structures (Schoonhoven and Eisenhardt 1987). As a result of environmentally induced changes, many firms are forced to change their internal structures and emphases to speed up the cycle from research to development to production. In some cases, the link between research and production must be strengthened, and the link between development and manufacturing tightened (Bailyn 1982; Schoonhoven and Eisenhardt 1987).

These changes can profoundly affect what the high-tech firm considers its criteria for success, how important stakeholders are to its mission, and the time frame for its work. As a high-tech firm goes from start-up through its evolutionary stages, it has the potential to increase its revenues to hundreds of millions of dollars and to expand its work force from a handful of people to thousands, in a period of five years (Bahrami and Evans 1987). This development requires some type of quick transition from an entrepreneurial start-up to a large, complex enterprise. Of course, many fledgling firms never survive either the liability of newness (Stinchcombe 1965) – because of which young organisations are particularly prone to failure – or the anatomy of the "living dead" (Bourgeois and Eisenhardt 1987), which describes those firms not sufficiently successful to be taken public, but not clearly failing enough to die.

Since the most fundamental currency of exchange in high-technology industries is knowledge – which resides in the professional and high-technology workers – spin-offs from established firms and the shifting of key people between firms can alter industry dynamics substantially (Bahrami and Evans 1987). Spin-offs in high-tech firms located in technopolii benefit from a large pool or experts, opportunities associated with growing markets, and the possibility of lacrative rewards from holding equity in these start-up firms (Bahrami and Evans 1987). The external environment associated with firms operating in technopolii provides not only a "laboratory" for quickly testing ideas but also a supply of venture capital that allows good ideas to become funded.

Thus, environmental conditions are bound to influence the work relationships, the procedures for career advancement, and the structures of these high-tech firms. Bailyn (1982) notes that as a firm responds to environmental changes – response being critical at the firm level – a series of four internal contradictions arise that interfere with the degree of career and work satisfaction of technical professionals. She maintains that these contradictions are not the result of ill will, but stem from the complexities of growth, development, and change. They do tend, however, to frustrate the professionals and high-technology workers to the point where they opt out of the employment contract. These contradictions have their roots in the characteristics of professional workers and are identified below (Bailyn 1982).

Organisationally Induced Contradictions

Autonomy Versus Control. As discussed in carlier, high-technology and professional workers aspire to operational autonomy and resist managerial attempts at control. Just as there are professionals who fit that mold, however, there are others who do not. There is evidence to suggest that the scientists demand strategic autonomy, whereas the engineers wish to retain control over day-to-day decisions. Hence, a firm must take into consideration that, for example, engineering professionals and successful engineering careers come in many different forms (Bailyn and Lynch 1983). Managers who wish to accommodate the career aspirations of their professional and high-tech work force must present choices of career growth opportunities (Miller 1986). For example, professionals who do not fit the stereotype of the scholar-scientist and who want to be given projects that are central to the firm's mission, with operational autonomy to work on those projects, do not need autonomy in choosing an assignment.

The key is in recognition. If the organisational reward system is accurately recognising differences in personnel, then ideally there will be organisational forms and practices that reflect those differences (Bailyn 1982; Bailyn and Lynch 1983; Bailyn 1985).

Stability Versus "Shake the Box." A common response to environmental pressures is to reorganise the firm, or "shake the box" periodically. Some high-tech firms regularly shake the box to get rid of complacency and stagnation. Others do so because of high uncertainty levels. The evidence to date is that in many research labs and high-tech firms, such reorganisations entail tremendous cost (Hannan and Freeman 1984). Professionals see little reason for many so-called reorganisations, particularly when project stability is threatened. From the organisation's point of view, however, combining functions and centralising procedures may make sense. But change for the sake of change makes very little sense. The key is in communicating and justifying the need for such changes, particularly as they impact the professional's work and career concerns.

Linear Versus Lateral Career Crises. Most workers in the United States aspire to promotion. Driver (forthcoming) refers to these workers as "ilinears"; they define career success sole in terms of upward mobility. Many professionals and high-technology workers are linears. Given the nature of most pyramid-shaped organisations, however, most employees are stymied in their quest for upward mobility after a certain point.

This reality includes the high-tech work force. Alternate career concepts exist, but little is done organisationally to accommodate the career aspirations of the many workers who prefer to work in their specialty areas, who do not aspire to upward linear movement. The key is in recognising different career concepts and in organisationally accommodating these differences through lateral promotions, transfers, or other methods. Most firms maintain that they want to accommodate their high-tech work force through attention to career needs. But most firms rarely investigate alternative structures for accommodating different career types.

Career Versus Work. A fourth contradiction arises when professionals position themselves so as to enhance their careers, but that positioning conflicts with the work itself. Bailyn (1982) notes that career advancement typically involves being visible to management, while effective work is often not visible to management. As with the other internal contradictions, some professionals will be career-oriented while others will be work-minded. Bailyn (1982) maintains that each type requires a different resolution. The professionals primarily interested in their technical work need alternative forms of recognition to keep them effective. These can come in the shape of different professional or career rewards, which may include placement on the dual ladder.

For those professionals and high-tech workers who aspire to hierarchical advancement, another dilemma occurs. If promotions occur too rapidly at the beginning of a professional's career, he or she runs the risk of future stagnation. Bailyn (1982) suggests that it might be better to slow down the promotions of younger professionals, while accelerating those of older career professionals. This is a reversal of the usual pattern. Workers who are somewhat ambivalent about their technical jobs—particularly the younger ones—should be encouraged to "try out" management, without making a long-term commitment or having important rewards withheld. Temporary assignments have had some success as a career reward for professionals.

Organisational Solutions

Managing a high-technology and professional work force involves recognition of the fact that contradictions exist. Most perspectives seem to differ on steps toward resolution of those contradictions. Four structural accommodations have beeen discussed regularly in the literature and are listed below. Each of these structural solutions has empirical support, but each has also experienced controversial implementation. Miller (1986) and others have reminded us that the primary solution is to present the professional with a choice of career growth opportunities, so that he or she does not have to aspire to management. Dual ladders, triple hierarchies, temporary assignments, and a variety of career management programs have been implemented with varying degrees of success. The following section examines the most popular solutions to accommodating the career concerns of professionals.

Dual Ladders

In an attempt to mitigate the professional-organisational conflict and to provide professionals with alternative career paths, some firms have implemented a dual-ladder structure. The dual ladder is a set of positions for professionals that is designed to be parallel to the managerial ladder, but with evaluation, control, authority, and advancement criteria appropriate for the technical professional. The objectives of using such a dual ladder are: to provide advancement opportunities for professionals who are unable or unwilling to ascend the managerial ladder; to provide compensation, recognition, and prestige equivalent to that of successful managers; to provide professionals with greater autonomy; and to create a set of positions with administrative duties light enough to not interfere with professional contributions (Hallenberg 1970; Healey 1960; Korhnhauser 1962; Secrist 1960; Miller 1986; Raelin 1987; Schriesheim, Von Glinow, and Kerr 1977). Figure 4.1 illustrates the single and dual-ladder hierarchy structures.

Figure 4.1. Single and Dual Hierarchies.

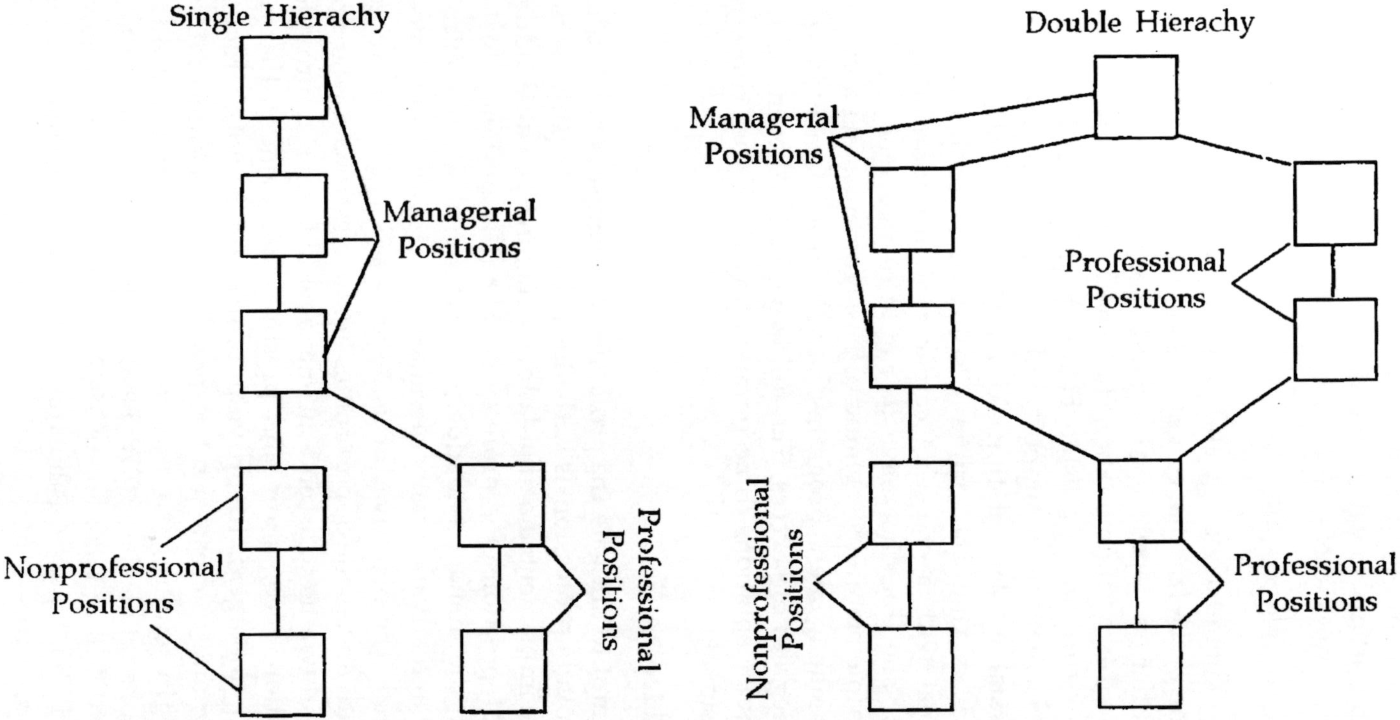

Source: Janet Schriesheim, Mary Ann Von Glinow, and Steven Kerr, "Professionals in Bureaucracies: A Structural Alternative", in *Prescriptive Models of Organisations*, ed. Paul Nystrom and William Starbuck, North-Holland TIMS Studies in the Management Sciences, Vo. 5 (Amsterdam: North-Holland, 1977), pp. 55-69.

The success of the dual ladder is mixed (Raelin 1987; Miller 1986). In reviewing dual-ladder programs in which professionals may choose either a technical or a managerial ladder, and both ladders carry the same prestige, salary, and responsibility, Raelin (1987) found that the concept is a viable one. He noted that pitfalls stem from improper operation rather than from distorted logic.

Miller (1986) notes that even the best dual-ladder programs receive about equal numbers of complaints from nonmanagerial professionals as from managers. Problems around the perception of unfair promotions predominate. Managers who are seen as managerial failures, but who are transferred and subsequently promoted on the technical ladder, can generate the sentiment that the technical ladder is a dumping ground for unsuccessful managers (Miller 1986).

It is very difficult to make both sides of the ladder really equivalent, although there are many reported successes. Westinghouse, IBM, and Goodyear, to name but a few, have claimed success with their dual ladders. Sacco and Knopka (1983) report that six criteria must be met for the dual ladder to be successful. The program must (1) have senior management support and commitment; (2) have credibility with employees; (3) be flexible and adapt to change; (4) define the levels of technical contribution at each rung in the ladder; (5) have a review process to assure quality; and (6) have a high profile, through publicity both inside and outside the firm.

Riggs (1983) maintains that equity in pay is not enough to ensure success; dual ladders must involve recognition as well as compensation with recognition being by far the more difficult to implement.

Triple Hierarchies

A variation on the dual ladder, the "triple hierarchy", provides three different advancement opportunities. The managerial hierarchy is available to those who want promotions into managerial positions. The dual ladder or technical ladder is available to those who want only professional and technical positions. The third ladder, called a "liaison hierarchy", is occupied by professionals in key administrative positions. They have regular technical duties, but also have hierarchical authority

Figure 4.2. Triple Hierarchy.

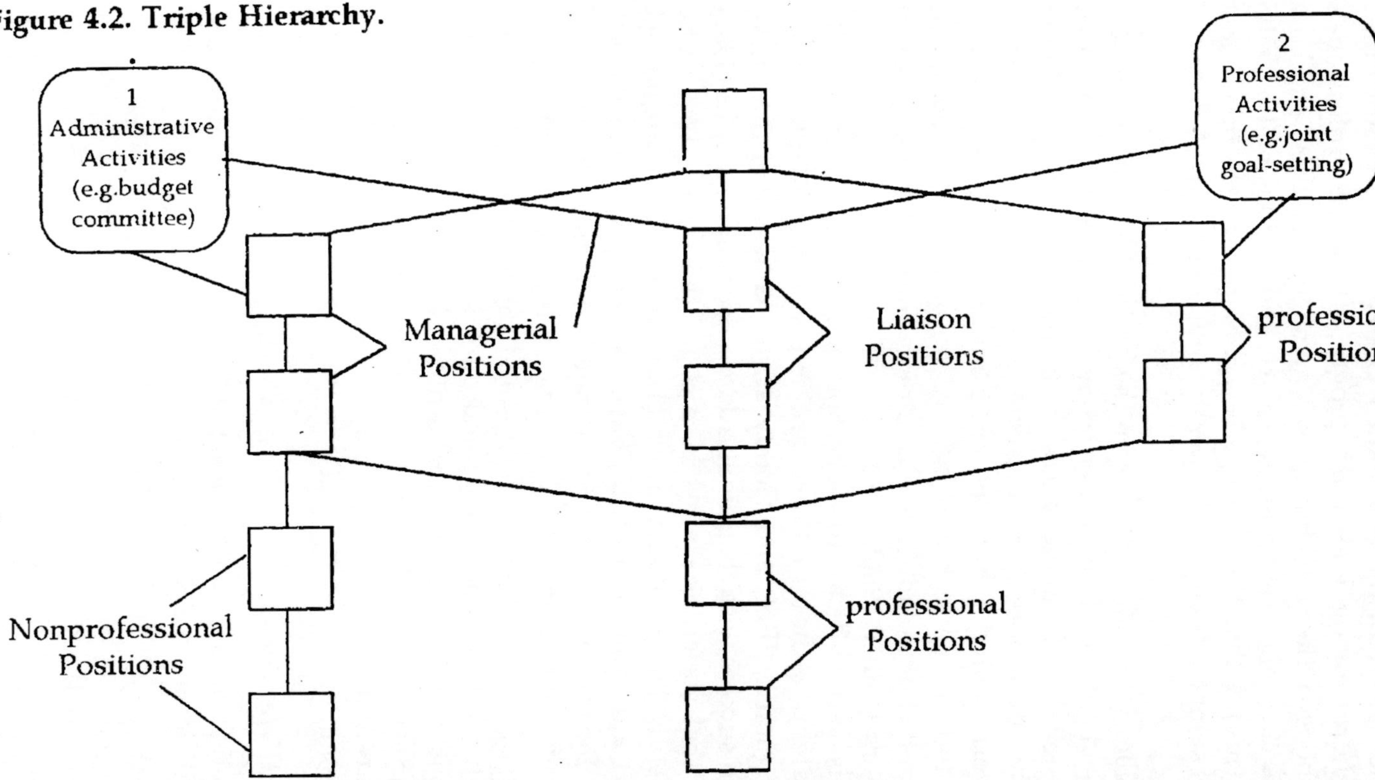

Source: Janet Schriesheim, Mary Ann Von Glinow, and Steven Kerr, "Professionals in Bureaucracies: A Structural Alternative", in *Prescriptive Models of Organisations*, ed. Paul Nystrom and William Starbuck, North-Holland TIMS Studies in the Management Sciences, Vo. 5 (Amsterdam: North-Holland, 1977), pp. 55-69.

over professionals in those areas where professional characteristics and organisational goals are most apt to conflict (Schriesheim, Von Glinow, and Kerr 1977). Figure 4.2 illustrates a triple hierarchy, with the managerial and technical ladders in place as well.

Table 4.1

Comparable Areas of Managerial and Liaison Authority

Managerial Hierarchy	*Liaison Hierarchy*
Purchasing of general clerical supplies and equipment	Purchasing of specialised technical supplies and equipment
Selection and training of office and low-level administrative personnel	Selection and training of professional and technical personnel
Supervision of nonprofessional managerial and office personnel	Supervision and coordination of professional activities
Responsibility for evaluation of office and low-level administrative personnel	Responsibility for conducting or coordinating professional employee performance appraisals
Distribution of resources required by nonprofessional employees	Distribution of resources required by professional employees
Budgeting for nonprofessional activities	Budgeting for professional activities

In those areas with high potential for conflict, managers have no authority. Such areas tend to vary by organisation. Table 4.1 briefly describes some areas where the liaison hierarchy would take precedence over the managerial hierarchy in most organisations.

In essence, "liaisons" represent the interests of both managerial and professional subgroups. They should be involved in processes such as controlling resources and planning functions, thus acquiring knowledge of the organisational constraints on resource allocation that affect the professionals. Similarly, liaisons can represent professionals on matters of company policy goal-setting, and resource allocation. This third ladder is, in effect, the buffer between the managerial and technical ladders.

Triple hierarchies have several advantages over dual-ladder systems. The most frequently stated reason for the failure of dual ladders is that professionals must rely on nonprofessionals for resources and services. The strength of the triple hierarchy is that it limits managerial authority to allocating resources and services to nonprofessionals only. Liaisons allocate resources and services to professionals, thus buffering both sides from one another.

Another advantage of the triple hierarchy over the dual ladder is that the triple hierarchy is more likely to equitably evaluate professionals, since evaluations and recommendations for promotion of professionals are made by liaisons, not by managers (Schriesheim, Von Glinow, and Kerr 1977).

A final problem – which is neither enhanced nor diminished by the triple hierarchy structural arrangement – is the continued perception of inequity across ladders, the perception that placement on the professional ladder is evidence of failure, or of an inadequate number of professional positions. This problem may emerge under the triple hierarchy, just as it does under the dual-ladder system; however, the triple hierarchy would not necessarily bring this problem about.

Temporary Assignments

As previously mentioned, temporary assignments can play an important role in an organisation employing high-technology and professional employees. These assignments may be to management or other kinds of tasks, to different phases of the R&D process – for example, from research to development – or to groups using different technologies (Bailyn 1982). These temporary or new assignments can alleviate stagnation, give recognition, and allow professionals to reapply their skills in different work situations. Bailyn (1982) notes that even the negative effects of constant reorganisations may be obviated when new organisation charts are seen to apply more to jobs than to the people doing the jobs.

There are, of course, inherent problems in managing within a fluid, flexible environment that utilises temporary assignments. There are costs associated with start-up for each job change, or each temporary assignment, as well as the possibility, as Bailyn (1982) says, that the reassigned person may not be able to handle the new job. These costs are reflected in the firm's tracking system. How is performance determined for professionals on temporary assignment? How are rewards allocated? who is ultimately responsible for these people?

When temporary assignments are performed at home on the computer, additional problems of control emerge (Metzger and Von Glinow forthcoming). The use of temporary assignments is not meant as a panacea; however, they are generally useful in the short term to alleviate specific problems.

Career Development Support

Career development has typically been the domain of the first-line supervisor (Walker and Gutteridge 1979) and has rarely been done well, particularly for professional and high-tech workers. Miller (1986) notes that career development support begins with training professionals and managers in the importance of the process of career management, which begins with improving the person-job fit. He claims that truly progressive high-tech firms begin career development programs as a part of the larger effort to improve productivity and reduce turnover.

Support for career development must be done within the prevailing culture of the firm. Thus, caring culture firms will likely support career development differently from exacting culture firms. Nevertheless, it seems that three types of support are fundamental to this process: top-management support; support for training of both managers and professionals in the methods of career management; and support through a firm's policies and procedures, which should allow the manager to sit down with the professional at least once a year for a career discussion.

Top-management support is not particularly controversial. The latter two—the training of managers and professionals in the methods, or "how-to" of managing their careers, and the career-thinking focus of a firm's policies and procedures—are somewhat controversial. For the past twenty years, U.S. firms have become much more attentive to career concerns (Dowd and Sonnenfeld 1984). This concern is manifested in a variety of career development activities. Some firms have formal career management programs; others try to incorporate some type of career-thinking into the annual performance appraisal. Most of these efforts fall into one of eight broad categories Arnold and Feldman 1986; Morgan, Hall, and Martier 1979; Feldman 1988). The following are some of the more commonly practiced career management programs for professionals and high-tech workers (Feldman 1988).

Career Information Systems. Many firms, including 3M and Lawrence Livermore Lab, actively disseminate information in-house about career opportunities. Jobs are posted, and professionals may nominate themselves for new positions. In some cases, information about career paths into key jobs is also provided.

Human-Resource Planning and Forecasting. Some firms—Rockwell International and Hewlett-Packard, among them—have computerised skills inventories of their workers. When new positions open up, the firm has a list of all the employees whose repertoire of skills fits the position description. Feldman 1988 notes that many firms now require their workers to prepare job replacement charts. Supervisors must document what training each of their subordinates would need for promotion, and their plans for providing that training (Hall 1976).

Career Counseling. Career counselors may be from the HR department or from outside professional services, or they may be professionals trained in the technical specialty of the individual requesting career counseling. In other words, this option covers a broad array of services. In house career counseling programs have increased dramatically within the last decade. Most career counseling begins with some type of self-assessment and with exercises designed to identify the important steps the employees must take to achieve his or her goals. At Lawrence Livermore Lab, technical and scientific professionals who hold graduate degrees in counseling psychology are employed as career counselors (Miller 1978).

Career Sequencing and Monitoring. As an alternative to random job placement, many organisations are beginning to sequence and monitor jobs for their high-tech work forces. In this way, career movements have a logic attached to them. In many high-tech firms, or in firms employing a great number of high-technology and professional workers, the dual ladder structurally serves this purpose. The burden is frequently placed on the manager, however, to ascertain strengths and weaknesses and to calibrate those on a reasonable career path for each employee.

Skills Assessment and Training. This type of career management program has its roots in the methodologies of the "assessment centers." pioneered by AT&T many years ago. This type of program is generally for mid to late career employees, whose skills may need to bolstering in some specific areas. To supplement this type of training, some in-house technical training of professionals may be utilised. Most companies today, in fact, offer some type of in-house training program to upgrade either technical or managerial skills. Tuition reimbursements are offered to many technical specialists, and to others seeking to upgrade their credentials, along with release time to pursue advanced degrees at local universities. The alternative concept of the "corporate college", however, is becoming more and more popular.

Career Development for Disadvantaged Groups. Many firms are seeking ways of helping employees who, historically, have been discriminated against in the United States. Enhanced recruitment and selection efforts, along with monitoring career movement for these minority employees, have become commonplace. Some firms even run career management seminars designed specifically for women, minorities, and late entrants into the work force (Morgan, Hall, and Martier 1979).

Career Development for Fast-Track Employees. For high-tech and professional employees who have the "right stuff", most firms are more apt to exert extra recruitment efforts and may monitor career progress as often as every six months. These valued employees receive counseling and training on an as-needed basis. Managers seem to be particularly sensitive to providing high potential workers with especially challenging work assignments.

Career Development Workshops for Supervisors. In most firms, the first-line supervisor is responsible for career development. Many firms are now expending considerable effort on training these supervisors in counseling, coaching, and career counseling. AT&T, for example, trains supervisors in job restructuring, joint goal-setting, career counseling, and performance appraisal skill development (Miller 1978).

Integrated Career-Thinking

It seems clear from the evidence so far that firms with successful career management programs for their high-tech and professional work force have integrated career development into their human-resource systems (Von Glinow, Driver, Brousseau, and Prince 1983; Feldman 1988). Further, these firms make good use of career rewards, which may even be based on length of service. Immediate-line supervisors are highly involved in career management techniques. Typically, there are periodic skills assessments, and these occur throughout the career of the professional.

Implicit in this process, of course, is realistic, credible feedback, given by someone trustworthy. Equally important is top-management support for these activities. It has been frequently documented that the most successful career development programs focus on job assignments and job design (Miller 1986) rather than on career advancement (Feldman 1988). Advancement is a promise that many firms simply cannot deliver; therefore, it is best to concentrate on career development for current job success. The concept of temporary assignments allows flexibility in job assignments and reward systems. As was previously discussed, different types of rewards can be linked to different factors, including age, skill level, and the like.

In summary, there are a variety of structures that can accommodate a professional's career growth and development. When we consider that career growth routinely emerges as an important source of loyalty to the organisation as well as an important reward, the structures that can enhance a professional's career development should be seriously considered. At a time when the high-tech revolution has deeply affected almost all industries, career development must be central.

5

Accounting and the Pursuit of Efficiency

Every society keeps the records most relevant for its major values. (Lazarsfeld, 1959: 108)

Accounting for the public sector has become a major issue for both discussion and action. In the last few years both the language and the practices of accounting have entered much more frequently and forcefully into debates about the efficiency, accountability and even scope of public sector activities. Appeals are now being made to the apparent inefficiency, lack of cost-effectiveness, unprofitability and waste associated with the public sector. Referring to the existing economic calculus, it is being said that we are now "living beyond our means', supporting that which is not 'economically viable', and either unable or unwilling to face 'the facts of economic reality'. Although there is a long history of investing in accounting mechanisms for recording, planning, controlling and making visible public sector activities, within a very short period of time indeed recent pressures for change have succeeded in challenging the adequacy of existing public accounts and management accounting practices. New demands are now being made for the practices of accounting to become even more implicated in public sector management.

Where have these pressures for change come from? What form do they take? And what are their implications? How, in other words, can we not only better understand the forces at work but also attempt to gain a more adequate appreciation of their consequences for both the technical practice of accounting and the conduct of business within the public sector?

Before focusing on these questions, however, it is useful to consider some of the ways in which existing accounting practices have become intertwined with quite substantive issues of public policy. For, like today, much of the power of the public accountings of the past derived from their ability to move beyond merely facilitating the operation of pre-given and relatively unproblematic forms of economic and financial management. Accounting has already been implicated in a more positive shaping and influencing of that which is regarded as problematic, the forms which public debates take and the options seemingly available for management and public action.

Accounting and Public Policy

Accounting records provide a way of freezing the decisions of the past (Bahmueller, 1981: 193). What was problematic and debated can become lost within the accounting archive. 'Facts' can thereby be created out of dissent and disagreement. An aura of the obvious and the unchallengeable can and does emerge out of the residues of past actions which accounting presents.

The significance of the ability of accounting to forge a domain of the factual in this way can be seen in the patterns of both relative and absolute performance of many public sector bodies. Past subsidies, allowances and provisions, decisions on transfer prices and payments, and the specific means used for their financing, play a significant role now in determining where current costs are incurred, continuing subsidies required and profits and losses both generated and shown. The relationships between past policies in the areas of defence, industrial development and regional support, all have current impacts of this type. Examples abound in the interplay of taxation, economic and social policies. For the National Coal Board, British Rail, London Transport and the Central Electricity Generating Board the patterns of present financial performance emerge out of a complex array of decisions of a social and political, as well as purely economic, nature. But those decisions give rise to accounting residues which can be and are used independently of the contexts out of which they emerged. Being 'profitable' or 'unprofitable', 'subsidised' or 'a drain on the Exchequer', can have a powerful contemporary significance. In this way accounting seems to provide a means of judiciously selecting the time-scale for comment and debate. The compelling obviousness of the present can overwhelm the contingencies of the past.

The fact that accounting, as we know it, provides a partial record of organisational choices and actions has also been of enormous importance. Organisational accounts both reflect and, in turn, influence the emphases that are given in public debates. Consequently, the economic has undoubtedly been made more visible than the social and the political, in many spheres of public life. Now, however, the imperatives of those economic 'facts' can be contrasted with the more questionable dictates of political ideology and social preference, illustrating, in the process, the powerful influence that the recording tools of the public domain can have. [...]

Accounting has also become implicated in the development of the institutional structures and linkages which today characterise the public sector. Particular forms of accounts have been used to buffer certain organisations from the dictates of government policy and intervention. 'Losses', for instance, have served as a pretext for price increases which have provided subsequent investment autonomy, sometimes on a very large scale; profits, similarly, have been used as evidence of both the granting of greater autonomy and its positive achievements. More frequently, accountings have served to tighten the relationships between different parts of the public sector. They have been used as a means of restraint; to constrain expenditures, actions and policies. The selective visibility created by organisational accountings has served to further the salience of imposed patterns of standardisation and uniformity. The information which they produce is used to monitor and evaluate the actions of others, and more frequent plans, budgets and reports can facilitate centralised control at the expense of local discretion.

All told, accounting is already centrally implicated in the institutional frameworks, language and patterns of power and influence that characterise the public sector. As a means of collecting and reporting selective patterns of information it has played a not insignificant role in the construction of public organisations and policies as we now know them. There are, however, yet further pressures for public sector accounting not only to change but also to expand its sphere of influence.

Pressures for Public Sector Accounting to Change

The pressures for the expansion and reform of public sector accounting are numerous, diverse and even conflicting in nature. Moreover, the emphasis given to particular factors can change remarkably over time, as recent decades have illustrated. In what follows, an attempt is made to outline only some of the main forces at work in recent debates in the area.

Changing Conceptions of the State. One of the major factors behind the current interest in public sector accounting is the changing view of the state that has entered political discourse in recent times. The legitimacy and value of at least some state actions and prengative are now being questioned from the perspective of a very different ideological stance. Indeed, a new way of examining and managing the state is emerging, and accounting is being implicated in that process.

Agencies of the state are now being asked to account for their aims, actions and achievements. Many more of their activities are coming to be seen in quite explicit economic terms. Cost and efficiency rather than effectiveness are being highlighted and debated. Information on economic consequences is being demanded. 'Value for money' has now entered the vocabulary of government.

[...] Economic calculations are now being seen as a way not only of reforming the management of the state but also of influencing the priorities which are gien in policy determination and decision-making. Accounting is quite explicitly becoming implicated in the construction of different views of the problematic, the desirable and the possible.

Accounting and Economic Restraint. Organisation tend to increase their investment in economic calculation and visibility during periods of restraint. In what has become known as 'newly poor behaviour' (Olofsson and Svalander, 1975), the constrained organisation places a renewed emphasis on costs, financial information and the calculus of economic decision-making. Mechanisms for enhancing economic visibility extend further into the organisation. Financial standards, budgets and plans become both more detailed and more subject to change. The organisation overall becomes more economically orientated, more influenced by economic calculation and, somewhat paradoxically (given that very frequently the economic difficulties emanate from without rather than from within), more orientated towards the seeming dictates of its own internal economic circumstances rather than the pressures of the world at large. [...]

During periods of economic difficulty, accounting and accountants have consistently expanded their sphere of influence in the UK. However, the relatively large British investment in the profession remains quite localised in its influence, having, until recently, much less of a presence in the service, financial and governmental sectors than in the area of manufacturing industry. Now, it seems, the current recession is providing a pretext for that to change, at least for the public sector. As the economic receives more emphasis in government, and as economic decision-making itself becomes more constrained, more and more demands are being made for the type of economic calculations that accounting provides.

The Search for Greater Efficiency. Continued economic restraint has given a new urgency to demands to improve the efficiency of management in the public sector. More and more accusations of waste, maladministration and inefficiency have been made. High staffing levels have been pointed out. The traditionalism and sluggishness of decision processes in the public sector is noted repeatedly. Although it is sometimes realised that the demands of public accountability and decision-making in a political context can serve to limit the extent to which concepts of efficiency derived from the private sector can be applied uncritically in the public domain, there nevertheless remains a feeling that much could be done to improve resource utilisation. Efficiency remains a very real and persuasive dream.

To this end, there is a renewed interest in importing into the public sector management practices developed in the private sector. Reference is made to the valuable roles that might be served by more adequate instruments for management planning and control. Appeals are made to the potential offered by improved costing procedures, more specific criteria for resource allocation, improved management information systems, investigations of administrative efficiency and better audits (which compare actual accomplishments with both original intentions and experience elsewhere). Such improved management practices, including those related to accounting itself, are seen as being able to assist in locating the inefficiencies of the past and ensuring that better performance is achieved in the future, not least by making public sector management and employees accountable for their actions and decisions.

Accounting and the Demand for Accountability. Appeals to the concept of accountability pervade many discussions concerned with the advance of accounting practice in the public sector. Accounting is seen as a way of both making visible and disciplining performance so that accountability can be demanded, policed and enforced.

A major impetas to the development of financial accounting in the private sector occurred when a separate cadre of managers came to be recognised as being accountable for their actions and performance to shareholders, the legally recognised owners of business. Since then, periodic crises of confidence have resulted: first, in more and more elaborate and detailed accountings of both organisational aims and achievements being demanded; and second, in the supply of such accountings by managers who have tried to maintain respect for their ability to manage the assets of others. Equally in the public sector, accounting has been implicated with the development of notions of stewardship and accountability. Accounting information has flowed from agenciess of the state to parliament and the public at large in recognition of the emerging constitutional requirement for the former to provide an account to the latter.

In the 1960s and early 1970s there were, in many Western countries, quite major pressures to expand the concept of accountability. In the name of social performance, environmental impact and the quality of working life, attempts were made to redefine the basis of organisational accountability to include aspects of performance broader than the purely economic. Related efforts were orientated towards expanding the information provided by the organisation in order to enable assessments to be made of its performance in new areas of concern. Notions of social, environmental and energy accounting and auditing were discussed and experimented upon. In the public sphere not unrelated developments were under way. Wider audiences started to demand the right to question the actions of the state. Not only was the state increasingly being asked to account for its actions and achievements, but greater demands were also being made for the right to assess public information, attend public meetings and more generally observe and interrogate the machinery of the state so that others might construct their own accounts of its performance. Concepts such as 'freedom of information' and 'the right to information' started to enter the language of political negotiation and debate.

However, in retrospect, it is interesting to note that most of these developments were much less significant in the UK than elsewhere. [In the UK] they did not result in any appreciable questioning of, let alone change in, concepts of either accountability or accounting. Ideas of wider accountings of the social remained peripheral to UK concerns. Nor was the traditional secrecy of the state effectively challenged in the name of wider rights to public information. Accounting maintained its emphasis on the economic, and disclosure, rather than access, remained the vehicle by which information flowed. The reasons for this relative lack of debate and change in the UK are little understood. However, it is possible to point to the continual dominance of the economic over the social in the UK, the emphasis that all sides of the political spectrum have put on the primacy of the ownership of assets (be they in private or public hands), rather than on other strategies for regulating their deployment and use, and the long history of constraints on the dissemination of information which still pervade our legal, administrative and constitutional systems.

From such a perspective perhaps we should not be surprised that recent discussions of the advance of public sector accounting in the UK continue to emphasize the narrowly economic. Efficiency and value for money, rather than effectiveness, are the focuses of attention. Equally, we can note how little attention continues to be given to strategies for the wider dissemination and use of information, accounting or otherwise. Although demands for more accounting are still permeated with the rhetoric of accountability, the latter continues to have quite a constrained meaning. Indeed, many recent discussions appear to emphasize the role that accounting can serve in advancing accountability within the machinery of the state, rather than between it and the public at large. Administrative rather than public accountability appears to be the problem at issue.

[...] Accounting is explicitly implicated in the development of quite strategic interests and concerns. Rather than emanating from the specifics of particular accountings, deficient or otherwise, current pressures for change have stemmed from views of the role which the particular might play in mobilising more general strategic arguments.

However, such strategic interests in accounting are now attempting to grapple with questions of the particular and the specific. A rhetoric of ceconomy, efficiency and value for money is now being used to call for a detailed concern with the specific accounting innovations that can service these wider ends.

The direction of change, from the general to the specific, has important implications for those interested in understanding and directing the practical process of accounting reform in the public sector. The generality, and indeed ambiguity, of notions such as efficiency and value for money must be recognised. For, although the ideas appeal to the comparison of inputs and outputs, and financial resources with their consequences, the delineation of those inputs, outputs, resources and consequences remains both a practically and conceptually difficult endeavour, not least in organisations which are complex, have little tradition of financial administration and economic record-keeping, and where outputs and consequences repeatedly arise in organisations different from those initiating the developments. In fact, very little is known about not only the practice of the new public accountings but also the wider impacts which might stem from such an intensification of economic visibility in the public domain. To date, accountings for efficiency and value for money have been advanced in the name of their presumed potential rather than their practical possibility or actual consequences.

On Examining the Practices of Accounting

In order to facilitate an examination of the practical consequences of public sector accounting developments, we now consider some of the ways of examining and questioning proposals for such accounting changes. Attention is directed towards the technical practices of accounting themselves, the ways in which they are embedded in organisations, and the wider issues to which extensions of accounting give prominence and significance.

Accounting as Technique. Given the ambiguity which pervades such notions as 'efficiency' and 'value for money' when used in public debate, it is always important to analyse proposals for the practical assessment of these concerns carefully and precisely. Only rarely can it be presumed that there will be a direct and unproblematic relationship between the issues of concern and their measurement in practice. More frequently, there will be a gap between the policies which mobilised interest and the specific accounting practices that result from them. Accounting, in practice, invariably requires a specification of detail and a reliance on other organisational practices and procedures that make the final assessments arrived at only partially dependent on the initial interest in them. When subsequently taken up and used in decision-making and policy formulation, practical accountings can, and do, have the potential to result in consequences very different from those originally envisaged for them.

Discretion often exists as to what inputs are deemed to be relevant, the costs that are assigned to the resources used, the outputs that are seen to flow from them, and their assessment in both financial and other terms. Issues of organisational interdependency will invariably arise, questions of presumed patterns of casual relationships will need to be debated, and proposals for specific valuations, weightings and assignments of priority will rarely be straightforward and unproblematic. Indeed, the difficulties of accounting in practice are such that it is often easy to arrive at a whole array of costs, efficiencies and value-for-money assessments. Many of these never see the light of day, however. Some are buried as a result of seemingly technical accounting choices; others fail to be recognised because of the dominance of particular organisational emphases and favoured theories of the determination of outcomes and consequences; and still others never emerge from internal discussions of 'the message to be presented'. [...]

Accounting and the Process of organising. Accounting has the potential to have organisational consequences beyond merely facilitating, in a technical manner, the processes of decision-making and policy formulation. By making visible what was previously unknown, it can open up different areas of the organisation for examination and debate. That visibility can also transcend different levels of the organisational hierarchy. What is accounted for can thereby shape the patterns of power and influence both within the organisation and without. Those with the power to determine what enters into the organisational accounts have the means to articulate and diffuse their values and concerns, and subsequently to monitor, observe and regulate the actions of those that are now accounted for. An expanded flow of information on organisational resources, capabilities and achievements can enable the monitoring, control and planning of organisational actions to be more readily abstracted from their execution. Management in other words, can become more centralised. New linkages can be drawn both within and between organisations. Different and more abstract criteria can be used for resource allocation. And opportunities can be created for new specialists to enter into the processes of decision-making and policy formulation. [...]

Accounting and the Creation of the Significant. The selective visibility which accounting gives to organisational actions and outcomes can play an important role in influencing what comes to be seen as problematic, possible, desirable and significant. Neither organisational participants, nor interested parties outside, can ever know the whole extent of organisational life. Direct observation can play a vital role in determining what is seen and valued. However, in organisational hierarchies and in those circumstances where geographical distance and organisational boundaries restrict what is directly visible, observation is soon supplemented and often superseded by that which is recorded. 'Information', both accounting and otherwise, then comes to play a significant role in determining what is known of the organisation and what is expected of it.

In such circumstances, those who influence what enters into the organisational accounts have a powerful and influential role. Some organisational disturbances are more likely to be seen as problematic than others. Some organisational options for change will be able to appeal more readily to supportive information and facts than others. Some criteria for the evaluation of change will likewise find it easier to relate to the partial mappings of the organisation that the incorporated into the accounting system. In these and other ways, not only can the emphasis given to different aspects of the organisation be changed, but also different values can more readily enter into decision processes, and appeals can be made to different legitimacies for action. The economic, for instance, can be given more attention than the social. The internal workings of the organisation can be emphasized rather than its external context. The immediate can be given priority rather than the longer term. Accounting, by shaping the realm of the visible, can have a major impact on the significance that is attached to both organisational life as it is and the directions of change which are considered desirable. Both the organisational landscapes of the present and the future are in part, at least, a creation of the accountings that are given of them.

A very conscious attempt has been made to emphasize the need to interrogate and understand proposals for accounting change in terms different and wider than those in which they are usually presented. The ambiguity and generality of the accounting desirable needs to be confronted by an insight into the specificity of actual accounting practice. This needs to be done in terms of its precise operationalisation, the impacts that it has on organisational functioning and the emphasis that it creates in discussions and debates. Just as accounting is called upon to serve more than the merely technical, so it needs to be evaluated in commensurate terms.

Accounting for Accounting

It is possible to examine developments in public sector accounting on numerous grounds and from a variety of different perspectives. In the discussion which follows, emphasis will be placed on just a few axes for questioning which, nevertheless, raise issues of quite widespread significance. Stemming from an appreciation of how the technical practice of accounting intermingles with the fabric of political and organisational life, the aim is to identify some issues which are worthy of consideration by a much wider audience than they attract at present.

Accounting, Technical Practice and the Realm of Politics. Accounting has the potential to create 'facts' out of the uncertain world of the past and even, in a planning context, the future. What was, and still is, debated and challenged can give rise to a residue of accounting calculations of what is costly, beneficial and of value. A world of the seemingly precise, specific and quantitative can, in this way, emerge out of that of the contentious and the uncertain.

A calculative priority can be given to the economic rather than the social. Costs, consequences and benefits can come to be divided into the defined and known, and the imprecise and intangible. In such ways accounting can create very different maps of organisational and social functioning. Particular emphases are given. Only certain chains of reaction are made visible. Only some consequences of actions enter into the world of the precise, the known and even the knowable. In part, at least, what comes to be known of organisational reality starts to be created by the accountings of it. A different view of what is central, and what is residual and peripheral, can start to be reinforced by the ways in which the calculations of accounting intertwine with the complex functionings of organisations as we know them.

Such changes in the visible are accompanied by other changes in organisational life. Expertise in the creation of particular organisational realities starts to emerge and be rewarded. Different legitimacies can come to be attached to arguments and viewpoints, depending on the extent to which they appeal to the domain of the newly factual. Quite specific calculative procedures for decision-making and resource allocation can come to be used in contexts where underlying disagreements remain.

Accounting, in other words, can become implicated in the creation of a domain where technical expertise can come to dominate political debate. By appealing to the centrality of the newly visible, be it the economic or whatever, an imperative for technical action can more readily be justified. What were previously seen to be problems of political priority can now start to be seen as requiring management guidance and expertise. We must now face the facts of the newly emerged reality. Rather than debating and arguing, we must appeal to those with expertise in the technical. Politics must stay at the door of public organisations. Within them, so it is said, planning, decision-making, resource allocation and the evaluation of performance must come to be seen in management terms. The emerging domain of the technically factual and necessary must be given priority over the domain of the political.

Such attempts to restructure the sphere of legitimate political debate and action have profound consequences for the nature of the society in which we live. Is it necessary, one wonders, for politics to be thus confronted by the domain of the technical? From what political strategies does this itself emerge And what are the wider consequences for political and social life? Just what might be at stake in such a juxtaposition of the rhetoric of efficiency with that of democracy? Is it really necessary, one wonders, for the enhancement of the legitimacy of the technical to be gained at the expense of the legitimacy of politics?

Of course, not all changes in public sector accounting raise such fundamental questions. Indeed, accounting itself can be used to mobilise political arguments and debates. The ambiguity of technical accounting practice is such that it often has an uncertain relationship to political practice. Nevertheless, both some specific proposals for accounting change and the general emphasis which together they place on the managerial and the economic, suggest that, at times, accounting developments do need to be seen in such wider terms. Although often masked by the language of the technical and the procedural, accountings can have quite profound consequences in the political sphere.

Accounting, Organisational Visibility and the Centralisation of Authority. Accounting can also become implicated in the creation of very different patterns of organisational influence and control. The selective patterns of visibility which it creates can enable the local to become known to the centre. Institutional bondaries can be made less opaque. Different patterns of local behaviour can come to be seen, compared and more readily labelled as conforming to, or deviating from, the dictates of the centre. Equally, the preferences of the centre can more easily become known to the local. Procedures for planning, budgeting and performance assessment can serve to both disseminate and make real the demands of the centre. Constraints on local behaviour can be imposed on the basis of the calculative visibility created by accounting systems. Specific behaviours can be monitored and more readily restrained. The local can, in this way, come to be managed as a part of the centre. Organisational interrelationships can become tighter. Discretion can more readily be specified and monitored. Indeed, the local can start to enter into the plans, policies and strategies of the centre so that the meaning of the distinction between the local and the centre can be radically changed.

Yet again, accounting can become implicated in the attainment of a set of consequences which extend far beyond the merely technical. Questions, therefore, can be, and perhaps should be, asked of the organisational and wider consequences of accounting developments.

Just who is made visible to whom? Are the patterns of visibility symmetrical of otherwise? Can only the centre observe the local? Or can the local-also observe the centre? Equally, what emphasis is placed on the forging of a visibility within the system of public administration, as compared with the creation of an external account? In other words, just what concepts of accountability (as distinct from accounting) are implicated in the process of accounting change?

Accounting and the Enhancement of Organisational Legitimacy. Accounting can also provide quite a direct basis for enhancing organisational legitimacy. Investments in rational organisational accounts and technical management procedures can be used to demonstrate to others that the organisation accepts the legitimacy of economic and technical bases for action and is seeking to further these ends. Accounts, plans, budgets and the practices of efficient management then become symbols of the organisation's commitment to efficiency both as an aim and a particular strategy of rational governance and management.

The manifestation of such accounting symbols need not result in their coupling to organisational action, however (Meyer, 1979; Meyer and Rowan, 1977). The display of the rational accounts may be orientated to those who ask questions of the organisation and seek to probe into its affairs from without, rather than to those who determine from within the organisation's course of events. So, somewhat paradoxically, if the investment in accounting provides sufficient evidence of the organisation's commitment to the course of events. So, somewhat paradoxically, if the investment in accounting provides sufficient evidence of the organisation's commitment to the course of rational economic and technical action, the discretion so gained might be used to uncouple organisational actions from the accounts which are made of them. Accounting might, in such circumstances, provide the freedom for the organisation to be unaccountable. By successfully appealing to the symbols of legitimate action, accounting might enable the internal affairs of the organisation to have a looser relationship to ethe external accounts of them.

Accounting and the Routinisation of Concern. Thus, the practices of accounting can come to be valued independently of the precise ways in which they intermingle with other organisational practices to influence the course of practical events. In any event, accounting, often stemming from more wide-ranging and ambiguous concerns, can have difficulty reflecting the specificity of both particular mobilising concerns and particular organisational phenomena, not least in the public sector. In addition, accounting can also come to function as a specialist area of activity in its own right. Technical questions of accounting can arise independently of the contexts in which it functions; accounting can be changed in the name of its own organisational bases and management rather than the wider concerns of the organisations in which it operates.

Such tendencies serve to detach accounting from the organisations in which it functions and the concerns in the name of which it was mobilised. Efficiency, for instance, can lose its force as the basis for accounting changes, to be replaced by a more procedural concern for accounting for efficiency. Similarly, plans can become more important than planning; budgets than the process of budgeting; and costing than the ascertainment of costs. A routine emphasis on accounting as procedure and technique can, at times, supersede accounting's initial concern for the issues in the name of which it was introduced and reformed. [...]

However, the tendency for accounting over time to emphasize the procedural and the routine, to the detriment of the managerial and the strategic, has recently been recognised as a problem in the industrial sector (Kaplan, 1985). There accounting's routine emphasis on the short-term economic has been seen to constrain the organisation's strategic vision and posture (Simmonds, 1983). Concerns have been expressed about the rigidity of the information and control practices which accounting has traditionally advanced. Accounting has been seen to emphasize the proliferation of routine techniques in the absence of a concern with the specific managerial consequences which they have. And quite active attempts are now being made in some parts of the private sector to reform accounting in the name of what it should be doing rather than what some now see as what it has done.

Accounting and Its Use. Accounting developments do not always lose contact with either the organisations or the missions which they seek to serve. Similarly, accounting does not have any automatic relationship to shifts in organisational legitimacy, the location of social power and influence, and what are seen to be legitimate or illegitimate bases for political action. Moreover, even when accountings of organisational actions and achievements do become intertwined with such substantive concerns, they do not necessarily have any automatic effects. Accountings can counter accountings: those provided by one organisation can confront those made by others. The routinisation of accounting can even limit the changes in organisational power that might stem from accounting developments. The legitimacy that a particular accounting helps to establish at the organisational boundary can protect rather than necessarily disrupt the internal political processes of decision making.

[...] The effects of accounting are determined by the uses that are made of it, the organisational and social roles which it is made to serve, the ways in which it intersects with other organisational and social processes and practices, and the resistances which its use engenders. Rather than being either a unitary or automatic phenomenon, accounting comes to function in a variety of very different ways in very different settings. And it is those ways and settings which influence the effects that it comes to have.

However, such a contingent view of accounting and its consequences does not deny that accounting can raise quite legitimate and significant questions at levels far beyond the purely technical. If for no other reason than this, accounting developments should be examined in a wider forum. Attempts should be made in this way to account even for accounting itself.

Accounting and That Which Happens in Its Name

Throughout this discussion an attempt has been made to demonstrate that the consequences of accounting do not necessarily have a close and automatic relationship with the aims in the name of which it is introduced and changed. For one thing, the aims that are expressed on behalf of accounting are general and often ambiguous. Stemming from political and managerial rhetoric, they are rarely expressed in terms of the specific operational and pragmatic questions which accounting must address before it can give rise to its technical procedures and practices. However, that gap between operationalization of accounting's aims can introduce quite significant elements of technical autonomy into the accounting process. These elements serve to distance the specific from the general to which it seeks to appeal. Equally significantly, accounting practices come to be enmeshed in wider organisational processes and concerns. The domain of the factual, which they create, gives rise to a visibility, emphasis and basis for governability that can enable the consequences of accounting to become both more pervasive and more independent of the original aims which might have been advanced on its behalf.

It is, therefore, always legitimate to seek to confront accounting with an analysis of the specific consequences which it has had. What has been changed in the name of accounting both within the organisation and without? What effects have attempts to increase efficiency actually had? What precisely has happened to costs, resources and outcomes? What organisational actions have been curtailed or expanded? What changes, if any, have been introduced into the power structure of the organisation and its processes of management and governance? And how do any such precise consequences of specific accountings relate to the missions and rationales which mobilised them in the first place?

Although such an examination should not be alien to the accounting perspective, accounting itself has only rarely been accounted for. The furtherance of accounting in the public sector could, however, provide an ideal context in which to ask questions of accounting; for its use in this sector can raise questions of a wider organisational, social and even political nature. Given this, perhaps we should use the current pressures for change as a basis for starting to account for accounting and to ask questions about what is actually achieved in the pursuit of efficiency.

The 'Implementation Problem'

One of the oldest topics in the study of organisations is the relation between policy and practice, the way general directives and programs adopted by legislatures, boards of directors, or top managements are executed, modified, and elaborated by administrative organisations. Contemporary forms of this interest are found in studies of program evalaution and policy implementation. Although there is no question that central policies affect organisational behaviour students of implementation frequently report complications in moving from adoption of a policy to its execution (Marshall, 1974). They often describe a scenario in which the wishes of central offices and policy-making bodies are frustrated by the realities of a decentralised administrative organisation (Levine, 1972; Pressman and Wildavsky, 1973; Edwards and Sharkansky, 1978; Hanf and Scharpf, 1978).

Two interpretations of implementation problems are common. The first interpretation attributes difficulties in implementation to bureaucratic incompetence. Sometimes bureaucracies are unable to accomplish the tasks they are assigned. The technical difficulties of organising for major programs are often substantial; the technical skills needed for a specific job may be unavailable (Allison and Halperin, 1971; Pressman and Wildavsky, 1973; Bardach, 1977). The second interpretation attributes difficulties in implementation to conflict of interest between policy-makers and bureaucratic agents, and thus to deficiencies in organisational control. [...]

The two interpretations are not mutually exclusive, and they are sensible. In the present chapter, however, we wish to suggest some limitations to such analyses and the importance of including an appreciation of the policy-making process in a discussion of implementation. [...] Analyses of the United States Congress, for example, suggest that 'the act of voting for legislation with appropriate symbolic meaning can be more important to legislators than either its enactment or its implementation (Mayhew, 1974). This is not because legislators are unusually hypocritical. It comes from practical concerns with maintaining electoral support and the substantial symbilic significance of political actions. Voters seek symbolic affirmations as well as mundane personal or group advantage. An interest in the support of constituents, whether voters or stockholders of clients, leads policy-makers to be vigorous in enacting policies and lax in enforcing them.

A desire to maintain the values, ideals, and commitments of an organisation or society can easily lead to a similar course (March and Olsen, 1976). Political actors, citizens as well as legislators, workers as well as managers, symbolise their virtues and proclaim their values by seeking and securing policy changes. Policies are not simply guidelines for action. Often they are more significantly expressions of faith, acknowledgements of virtue, and instruments of education. Individuals and groups support (often with extraordinary vigor and at considerable cost) the adoption of policies that symbolise important affirmations, even where they are relatively unconcerned with the ultimate implementation of the policies. As Arnold (1935:34) observed: 'It is part of the function of Law to give recognition to ideals representing the exact opposite of established conduct. Most of the complications arise from the necessity of pretending to do one thing, while actually doing another.'

Cases of such clear intentionality are, however, only a minor part of the story. They dramatise the limitations of talking about 'implementation problems', but they do not define those limitations. We will argue the more general point that an understanding of implementation cannot be divorced from an understanding of the processes that generate policies, and that some conspicuous feature of policy-making contribute directly to the phenomena we have come to label as problems of implementation.

Bureaucracies as Instruments of Policy

Despite the pervasiveness and effectiveness of bureaucratic organisation, there are ample grounds for doubting that a modern administrative agency will fulfill any policy directive that it might be assigned. For example, bureaucratic inability to cope with the size or scope of new responsibilities has been used to explain the difficulties of some business organisations implementing policies that lead them into foreign markets and of military organisations implementing policies that ask them to fight limited wars. One typical situation in the public sector involves the implementation of new national programs through local departments or bureaus seemingly illequipped to administer them.

Consider, for example, Sutherland's (1975:74-6) portrayal of problems in implementing the Elementary and Secondary Education Act of 1965 in the United States:

> Although some state agencies in 1965 were considered to be well managed, most were thought to lack sufficient personnel to supervise existing state programs or the capability to assume new responsibilities needed to meet future educational neeeds. Although all state departments of education had professionals capable of providing consultative and technical service to local educational agencies, the number of staff members available on a full-time basis was limited only one fifth of the states had two or more supervisors of teacher education and 15 did not have a part-time employee for this activity. One-third of the states provided no services or supervision of school libraries. Twenty-nine did not provide for the supervision of industrial arts programs and the remaining states had only a supervisor of vocational education. Four state agencies had no full-time staff members to consult with local school systems for special education and only 13 had one or more full-time consultants for the development of programs for the gifted...Persons in possession of skills and the training to conduct research, evaluate findings and test and implement new instructional programs were also needed by state educational agencies. Although more than two-thirds of the state agencies had departments that included to word 'research' as a part of the title, only 108 persons were employed for research purposes, and nine state departments of education listed no research personnel.
>
> [...] The idea that implementation is made difficult by the posibly unavoidable, and certainly ubiquitous, problems of bureaucratic and individual incompetence is found in many analyses of modern administrative agencies. Logistic complications are not solved in time. Coordination among agencies is not accomplished, even when there is no

> significant conflict among them. Materials, plans, and people are not available when needed; personnel are not trained properly or are given inadequate instructions or supervision (Allison and Halperin, 1971).

Agencies are sometimes sloppy, disorganised, inadequately trained, poorly staffed and badly managed; but gross incompetence is not required to produce significant bureaucratic inadequacy. Some tasks are not feasible; some policies are ill-suited to administrative agencies. Moreover, it is possible to recognise the considerable individual and organisational skills represented in a bureaucracy and still observe a mismatch between a particular organisation and a particular task. For example, the United States Forest Service has had difficulty playing the role of a narcotics police force in national forests.

These difficulties are frequently further complicated by a need to coordinate several different organisations in order to implement a single general policy (Elmore, 1975; Hanf and Scharpf, 1978). Central policy may require coordination among organisations with sharply contrasting objectives, styles, or normal activities. Managing several relatively autonomous groups often demands capacities beyond those of elaborate bureaucratic structures, not to mention the largely ad hoc structures that are sometimes used. Policy-makers often ignore, or underestimate considerably, the administrative requirements of a policy, and thus make policies that assure administrative incapacity.

The problems of incompetence are paired with problems of control. Administrative organisations are neither reliably neutral nor easily controlled. They seem persistently to modify policies in the course of implementing them. Descriptions of such local adaptations tend to overestimate the extent to which official policy, as interpreted by interested observers, can be equated either with the public interest or with the intentions of legislatures (Lynn, 1977). They are likely to picture national officials, top management, or major policy-makers as defending general interests against the predations of local officials, subordinates, and special interest. The core idea, however, does not depend on that particular representation of a morality play. Whenever an agent is used to execute the policy of a principal, control problems arise. The problems are endemic to organisation and have been extensively discussed in the literature on organisations (March and Simon, 1958; Crozier, 1964), as well as in treatises on optimal contracts, incentive schemes, and theories of agency (Hirschleifer and Riley, 1979).

Bureaucracies appear often to be thoroughly political, responding to claims made in the name of subunits, clients, and individual organisational actors. Political processes continue as policies filter through a bureaucracy to first-level administrative officials. Agencies adopt projects and implement programs in response to political pressure or financial incentives; they exercise discretion in order to improve their local position or address specific problems of interest to them; they interpret policy directives in ways that transform their prior desires into the wishes of policy-makers. For example, the Fort Lincoln project, seen by political leaders as a way to help poor people escape city slums, was converted into a program to build model communities and to try out the newest ideas in community planning (Derthick, 1972).

In dealing with organisational actors, policy-makers find it hard to ensure that incentives for following official policy are adequate to overcome incentives to deviate from it (Christie, 1964). Organisations, their clients, and their subunits pursue political tactics seeking renegotiation of policies and practices. Since from the point of view of most other groups and institutions, any new policy announced by policy-makers is primarily an opportunity to pursue their own agenda, those responsible for implementing policy have constitutents who seek deviations from policy. Some parts of any administrative organisation will have incentives for pursuing objectives that deviate from any policy that might be adopted (Downs, 1967).

The difficulties in coordinating the agendas of multiple actors are compounded by the way political and organisational actors move in and out of the arena in response to various claims on their attention (March and Olsen, 1976). An organisation is pressed to meet the inconsistent demands of a continually changing group of actors. Pressman and Wildavsky (1973) suggest some reasons for the inconstancy of attention: actors may find their commitments to a policy incompatible with other important commitments; they may have preferences for other programs; they may be dependent on others who lack the same sense of urgency; they may have differences of opinion on leadership or proper organisational roles; they may be constrained by legal or procedural questions or demands. In general, a shifting pattern of demands for attention made on the individuals involved in and around an organisation tends to make the climate of implementation unstable in many small ways that cumulatively affect the course of events (Kaufman, 1981).

Programs for Reform of the Policy Process

Because it is part of classical administrative dogma, and because bureaucratic organisations do, in fact have a rather impressive record for successfully coordinating large numbers of people in service of policies imposed from outside, it is persistently tempting to picture administrative agents as natural implements of prior policy. They are made innocent by an act of will or good management. In this spirit, problems of implementation lead to proposals to increase competence and control by hiring new personnel, developing new training or procedures, improving accountability, and providing new incentives. For example, foreign service organisations may respond to diagnoses of incompetence by increasing the length of service at a particular station for individual officers; they may respond to diagnoses of lack of control by requiring more frequent rotation of officers through stations. Implementation failures may lead to new organisational forms, for example divisional management; to new investments, for example in management information systems; to new routines, for example evaluation studies; or to new personnel, for example new top executives.

Such changes are intended to make an organisation into a competent, reliable agent, executing a wide range of possible policies. They picture the problems of implementation as problems of securing neutral administrative compliance with prior, exogenous policies. This view of administration has, however, long been in disrepute among students of organisations. It suggests mroe clarity in the distinction between policy-making and administration than can usually be sustained; and it leads to a mechanistic perspective on the management of organisations that seems likely to be misleading. Trying to keep administrators innocent may, of course, simply reflect an instinct to use unachievable aspirations as a means of achieving less heroic, but admirable outcomes (March, 1978. 1979); but it tends to delusion. Consequently, many sophisticated observers of organisations take a more strategic posture with respect to designing administrative organisations.

Suppose we accept the proposition that bureaucracies are limited instrumentalities, that there are constraints on our abilities to make them more competent or to avoid the demands of self-interest. Then implementation problems are attributed not to characteristics of organisations—which are taken as essentially intractable—but to the naivety of policy-makers. In this view, policy-makers do not specify objectives clearly enough (Lochen and Martinsen, 1962; Jacobsen, 1966; Lowi, 1969; Sabatier and Mazmaniar: 1980), provide inadequate resources, fail to build a proper administrative organisation, fail to consult with affected groups, or have too high expectations. Such a strategic vision leads to recommendations to improve the policies, make them clearer and more consistent with the attitudes of the groups involved, and strengthen the incentives and capabilities for bureaucratic conformity to policy directives.

[...] Many problems in implementation might be avoided if policy-makers made less ambiguous policies and designed simple procedures that protected their intentions from the inadequacies and self-interest of administrative agencies. Rather than expecting to change the character of administrative organisations, we might design strategic policies, quasi-price systems, and incentive contracts that are likely to lead to desired ends even when executed by administrative organisations that are neither perfect nor neutral.

These efforts to increase the sophistication of policy-makers in dealing with administrative agencies, like earlier attempts to improve the competence and reliability of the agencies, are vital to good administration. Without a struggle to link policy and action, any social system suffers. However, we want to argue that the problems of implementation are obscured by the terminology of implementation, even in its more sophisticated forms, that discussions of implementations assume a coherence in policy objectives that rarely exists. Understanding administrative implementation cannot be separated from understanding the ways in which policies are made and the implications of the policy-making process for administrative action.

Policy-Making and Policy Ambiguity

Proposals for implementations reform treat policy—or policy objective—as given. They assume that policy goals and directives are (or can be) clear, that policy-makers know what they want, and that what they want is consistent, stable, and unambiguous. The assumptions are similar to assumptions about preferences made in standard decision theory, and they have some of the same advantages (Raiffa, 1968). They made administration, like decision-making, a difficult technical job of optimisation, subject to prior exogenous policies established by legitimate authority. They also have many of the same disadvantages (March, 1978; Elster, 1979; Cronbach *et al.*, 1980).

In particular, the assumptions are often not true. They are frequently false in a way that makes the concept of implementation not only inaccurate as a portrayal of organisational reality, but often an inappropriate base for organisational reform. For example, the frequent advice that policies should be clear seems to assume that policy-makers can arbitrarily choose the level of clarity of a policy, that policies are ambiguous because of some form of inadequacy in policy-making. Such a view ignores what we know about the making of policies. In fact, policies are negotiated in a way that makes the level of clarity no more accessible to arbitrary choice than other vital parts of the policy.

Forming a coalition in order to support a policy, whether in a legislature or a boardroom, involves standard techniques of horse-trading, persuasion, bribes, threats, and management of information. These are the conventional procedures of discussion, politics, and policy formation. They are well conceived to help participants form coalitions, explore support for alternative policies, and develop a viable policy. Much of the genius of modern organisational leadership lies in skills for producing policy from the conflicting and inchoate ideas, demands, preconceptions, and prejudices of the groups to which organisational leadership must attend. At the heart of several of these techniques for achieving policies, however, are features that make implementation problematic.

Adopted policies will, on average, be oversold. Even unbiased expectations about possible policies will lead to bias in the expectations with respect to those that are adopted. Since proposed programs for which expectations are erroneously pessimistic are rarely adopted, the sample of adopted programs is more likely to exhibit errors of over-optimism than of over-pessimism (Harrison and March, 1984) Inflated expectations about programs that are successful in gaining support from policy-makers make subsequent disappointment likely. Thus, great hopes lead to action, but great hopes are invitations to disappointment. This, in turn, leads both to an erosion of support and to an awareness of 'failures of implementation.'

Such a structural consequence of intelligent decision-making under conditions of uncertainty is accentuated in situations of collective choice. Competition for policy support pushes advocates to imagine favourable outcomes and to inflate estimates of the desirability of those outcomes. Developing and communicating such expectations are a major part of policy discussions. Expectations become part of the official record, part of collective history, and part of individual beliefs. Others will, of course, try to deflate the estimates of advocates; but the advocates usually write the stories for their preferred policies and often come either to believe them or to be commited publicly to them. Tactical supporters of policies (i.e., those who support policies for reasons extraneous to their content) do not resist being misled. Extravagant claims justify their support and provide a basis, if one is ever needed, for claims that they are duped.

In addition, the centripetal processes of policy-making exaggerate the real level of support for policies that are adopted. Although commitment to a policy or program in its own right may be important for some coalition members, few major policies could be adopted without some supporters for whom the policy is relatively unimportant except as a political bargain. They may be persuaded to join a coalition by a belief the policy is sensible, by claims of loyalty or friendship, or by a logroll in which their support is offered in trade for needed support on other things in which they have a direct concern. There is no assurance that such groups and individuals will be equally supportive of its implementation. Except in so far as their continued active support is a part of the coalition agreement, and such extended coalition agreements are difficult to arrange and enforce, supporters will turn to other matters. Consequently, a winning coalition can easily be an illusion (Sactren, 1983).

Finally, one common method for securing policy support is to increase the ambiguity of a proposed policy (Page, 1976). It is a commonplace observation of the legislative process that difficult issues are often 'settled' by leaving them unresolved or specifying them in a form requiring subsequent interpretation. A similar observation can be made about policies in armies, hospitals, universities, and business firms. Particularly where an issue is closely contested, success in securing support for a program or policy is likely to be associated with increasing, rather than decreasing ambiguity. Policy ambiguity allows different groups and individuals to support the same policy for different reasons and with different expectations, including different expectations about the administrative consequences of the policy.

Thus, official policy is likely to be vague, contradictory, or adopted without generally shared expectations about its meaning or implementation. Aubert, in is study of the enactment of a Housemaid Law in Norway (Aubert 1969:125), discusses the apparent anomaly of legislation that paired a policy proclaiming the protection of household workers with a set of procedures for redress that were effectively inaccessible to victims:

> What is pretended in the penal clause of the Housemaid Law is that effective enforcement of the law is envisaged. And what the legislature is actually doing is to see to it that the privacy of the home and the interest of housewives are not ignored...The ambivalence and the conflicting views of the legislators, as they can be gleaned from the penal clause, appear more clearly in the legislative debate. A curious dualism runs through the debates. It was claimed, on the one hand, that the law is essentially a codification of custom and established practice, rendering effective enforcement inessential. On the other hand, there was a tendency to claim that the Housemaid Law is an important

> new piece of labour legislation with a clearly reformatory purpose, attempting to change an inacceptable status quo...The crucial point here is the remarkable ease with which such apparently contradictory claims were suffused in one and the same legislative action, which in the end received unanimous support from all political groups.

In this way, the ambiguity of a policy increases the chance of its adoption, but at the cost of creating administrative complications. For example, Øyen (1964) observed that the ambiguous text of a Norwegian welfare statute was simultaneously a necessary condition for the unanimity of its political support and a basis for considerable administrative discretion. As a policy unfolds into action, the different understandings of an ambiguous political agreement combine with the usual transformation of preferences over time to become bases for abandoning support, deploring administrative sabotage of the program, or embracing a special fantasy of what the policy means. As a result, many coalition members can easily feel betrayed; and observers can casily become confused.

In the long run, of course, political institutions learn from their experience. Administrative agencies seem likely to adapt to a history of ambiguous, contradictory, and grandiose policies by an administrative posture that tends to emphasize creative autonomy. They learn to establish independent political constituencies, to treat normal policies as problematic (or at least subject to interpretation), and to expect policy-makers to be uncertain, or in conflict, about the expected consequences of a policy, or its importance. They come to realise that they cannot escape criticism by arguing that they were following policy but must develop an independent political basis for their actions.

Similarly, policy-makers learn from their experiences with administrative agencies. As administrative practices become flexible, it becomes easier to use policy ambiguity as a basis for forming coalitions. It becomes plausible to attribute failures in programs to failures in implementation and thus to avoid possible criticism for mistakes. Policy ambiguity encourages administrative autonomy, which in turn encourages more policy ambiguity. Thus, it is not hard to see why we might observe organisations functioning with only a loose coupling between policies and actions, between plans and behaviour, and between policy-makers and administrators (March and Olsen, 1976; Weick, 1976).

The Concept of Implementation

The terminology of implementation conjures up a picture of clear, consistent, and stable policy directives waiting to be executed. It encourages us to think that a reasonable and responsible person can easily measure the discrepancy between policy and bureaucratic action, that the discrepancy can be attributed to some properties of the organisation (e.g. its competence and reliability) or to some properties of the policy (e.g. its clarity and consistency), and that the properties of the organisation and the properties of the policy can be chosen arbitrarily and independently in order to reduce the discrepancy.

As we have noted, studies of policy-making cast doubt on such a characterisation. The implementation of policies is frequently problematic; but the difficulties cannot be treated as independent of the confusions in the policy. Those confusions, in turn, cannot be treated as independent of the ways in which winning policy coalitions are built. Policies are frequently ambiguous; but their ambiguities are less a result of deficiencies in policy-makers than a natural consequence of gaining necessary support for the policies, and of changing preferences over time. Conflict of interest is not just a property of the relations between policy-makers on the one hand and administrators on the other; it is a general feature of policy negotiation and bureaucratic life. As a result, policies reflect contradictory intentions and expectations and considerable uncertainty.

It may be tempting to deplore a policy process that sometimes seems to restrict us to a choice between inaction and ambiguity, and to wish for some alternative system in which policy agreements would be clear and their execution unproblematic. But that concern should be paired with an awareness of the complications. The problems involved in establishing and maintaining an effective policy-making and an administrative system that provides responsiveness, coherence, and symbolic affirmation of social values have occupied philosophers and managers for long enough to suggest that they are not trivial. Certainly, contemporary theories of policy-making and administration have not solved them. Nor have we. As a preface to such an effort, however, we have argued that the terms of discourse for discussing policy-making and implementation are misleading. Any simple concept of implementation, with its implicit assumption of clear and stable policy intent, is likely to lead to a fundamental misunderstanding of the policy process and to disappointment with efforts to reform it.

6

Organisational Culture

The study of organisational culture—the proposition that organisations create myths and legends, engage in rites and rituals, and are governed through shared symbols and customs—is much in vogue. Although the reasons for this are not entirely clear, two issues deserve mention. (1) the effect of political, ideological and socioeconomic factors on social theory; (2) the related issue of the scholarly and ideological implications of the selective borrowing of key concepts from one discipline by other fields of study.

The present preoccupation with organisational culture is probably related to socioeconomic factors in Western society. Most Western countries have experienced a dramatic downturn in their economies. This, in turn, has helped to emphasize the structural inequalities inherent in these societies and has placed the structure of Western capitalism under severe pressure. It is probably no accident that many scholars are emphasizing cultural problems—particularly where cultural problems are naively operationalised in terms of 'people problems'—at a time when the structures of many Western institutions are under strain.

Some social theorists use the term 'culture' to embrace all that is human within the organisation. They emphasize culture, either consciously or unconsciously, in such a way as to blur or hide problems and contradictions inherent in the social structure. Of course, both an organisation's culture and its structure are socially created; but that is not what is at issue here. The problem with some studies of organisational culture is that they appear to presume that there exists in a real and tangible sense a collective organisational culture that can be created, measured and manipulated in order to enhance organisational effectiveness. The link between 'culture' and 'effectiveness' has become, recently, quite pronounced, and studies incorporating in their title such phrases as the 'culture of school effectiveness', or the 'culture of corporate effectiveness' abound. It is implied that an ineffective organisation can be made effective—a school can produce the 'model citizen', that is, one who can find employment, and the corporation can enhance its profit margin—if an unhealthy organisational culture can be supplanted with a healthy one. The problem is one of changing people's values, norms and attitudes so that they make the 'right' and necessary contribution to the healthy collective 'culture' despite (or in ignorance of) any inherent conflict of individual and group interest or the way in which power, authority and control are structured in the organisation.

Areas of study, such as the study of complex organisations—including educational and corporate administration, management studies, and human relations and interpersonal dynamics—are influenced by concepts that filter down into the ranks of their practitioners from older, well-founded disciplines. The idea of culture in organisations is a concept borrowed mostly from anthropology, although some sociologists, such as Durkheim, have also been influential.

There is nothing wrong with one discipline borrowing concepts from another discipline; this process has resulted in important theoretical imovations. However, there is a danger that, when one area of study borrows key concepts from other disciplines, the concepts become either stereotyped or distorted in the transfer. Also, when concepts are borrowed from other disciplines, they may not be borrowed *into:* that is, rather than accepting an entire 'package'—which may include the historical debates surrounding the 'proper' uses of the concepts—people only select aspects of the concepts that suit their interests and thinking at a particular time. This may result either in a slanted and biased application of the concepts or a dilution of their original analytical power.

The concept of organisational culture can be a powerful analytical tool in the analysis and interpretation of human action within complex organisations. Alternatively, it can be misused to reify the social reality of organisational life. It may be timely to have a close look at some of the ways in which the concept of 'culture' has been used in organisational research, paying particular attention to questions concerning what aspects of the concept of culture have been borrowed from anthropology and, to a lesser extent, sociology. It seems that much of the use of culture as a unitary concept expressing, on the one hand, social cohesion and integration, and on the other, organisational effectiveness, is the result of the transfer of the concept of culture to organisational analysis from a particular anthropological and sociological theoretical tradition, i.e., the 'structural-functional', theoretical paradigm.

[...] There is a growing body of literature that critically assesses the study of organisational culture, and it is likely that the debate surrounding the 'proper' use of the concept of culture in organisational analysis will continue for some time (see, in particular, Allaire and Firsirotu, 1984; Gregory, 1983; Smircich, 1983). This chapter contributes to the debate in three limited ways. First, it briefly reviews a few of the consequences of the selective borrowing of the concept of culture. The purpose here is not to debunk past studies of organisational culture, but to attempt to illustrate some of the political and ideological as well as the scholarly effects of viewing culture from a particular theoretical perspective. The chapter then attempts to disentangle the subtle difference between an organisation's culture and its social structure, concluding with a brief discussion of some 'sub-concepts' that comprise the idea of culture. Culture, as a total concept, is too all-ambracing. It needs to be dissected into manageable proportions so that it can be used in the interpretation of observed behaviour.

The Concept Borrowed

Some recent studies of organisational or corporate culture have been undertaken by what Turner (1986), drawing on Ott's (1984) terminology, calls 'pop cultural magicians', 'tricksters' who make their living by convincing North American and European corporate executives that they can equal the productivity of Japanese industry through the mechanical manipulation of organisational symbols, myths and customs. Such studies are not much concerned with theory of any sort, but seize upon fads in the realm of ideas. However, many 'honest grapplers'

(Turner, 1986) in their approach to corporate culture have produced studies that also seem unduly linked to the interest of management and which promulgate the idea that 'culture' is the collective consciousness of the organisation, 'owned' by management and available to management for manipulation. An attempt will be made to illustrate the effects of these weaknesses on the study of corporate culture, not by questioning the integrity of individual researchers, but through examining the theoretical basis on which the idea of corporate culture rests. The argument will explore three interrelated themes:

1. Organisational theorists—particularly, though not exclusively, those belonging to the human relations and related schools—have not considered the multiplicity of theories of culture, but have borrowed the concept of culture from only one anthropological tradition: structural functionalism.
2. Although: theories of organisational or corporate culture have their 'roots' in structural—functionalism, they have also 'mutated' in the process of application.
3. The equating of corporate culture with a 'natural' force for social integration within the organisation—with a unitary organisational collective consciousness that can both be measured and manipulated -- seems to flow from the structural-functional tradition from which the concept is borrowed.

[...] The purpose of this chapter is not to ground contemporary criticisms of corporate culture studies in past criticisms of structural-functionalism. Rather, the intention is to illustrate how studies of corporate culture, because of the structural-functional theoretical legacy, tend to ignore or gloss over inherent conflicts and important structural features of the organisation, particularly the structure of power and conflict, structured inequality and the significance of the structure of 'class cultures' (see Turner, 1986). Later in the chapter an attempt will be made to build the concept of structure and conflict back into a theory of corporate culture.

The structural-functional theoretical framework has had a profound influence on all aspects of the study of complex organisations. Its influence on the concept of organisational culture is particularly notable, which is not surprising since 'structural-functional' theory has its roots in the development of British social anthropology in the 1920s, 1930s and 1940s (Kuper, 1973). While Talcott Parsons transported structural-functionalism across the Atlantic, the British social anthropologists – themselves influenced by the French sociologist Emile Durkheim – gave birth to the theory. Out of the many conceptualisations of culture available, social theorists have been prone to seize – sometimes somewhat uncritically – upon Durkheim's idea of the collective consciousness and upon Radcliffe-Brown's notion that 'cultural patterns are crystallised in social structure "as institutionalised and standardised modes of behaviour and thought whose normal forms are socially recognised in the explicit or implicit rules to which members of a society tend to conform' (Keesing, 1974:83). Several studies of organisational culture seem to assume that 'culture' is a unifying force within the organisation, that there exists a universal homogeneous culture, and that the task for the researcher is to discover it. A few examples will help illustrate the point.

Kilmann (1982:11) refers to culture as 'the collective will of members'; it is 'what the corporation *really wants* or what *really counts* in order to get ahead'. According to Schwartz and Davis (1981:33) culture is 'a pattern of beliefs and expectations shared by the organisation's members' that create 'norms that powerfully shape the behaviour of individuals and groups in the organisation'. Kilmann *et al.* (1985a:2) claim that their edited book *Gaining Control of the Corporate Culture* represents the 'State of the art' of corporate culture' and that the contributors are 'those who are at the leading edge of this topic'. In chapter after chapter, definitions of culture are provided that stress the internalisation of norms, social integration and stability, that link culture firmly with the interests of management, and that treat culture as the collective will or consciousness of the organisation. [...]

Gaining Control of the Corporate Culture contains interesting and valuable information on aspects of the operation of various corporations, but except for one or two chapters, the theories of culture used by the contributors rest on the premise that the norms, values and beliefs of organisational members are factors that create consensus, predict behaviour and create unity. This leads to conclusions that are little more than statements about management's responsibility to reward positive behaviour and attitudes, to foster the self-esteem and self-confidence of organisations' members, to encourage allegiance to organisational goals and missions, to inform members of the need for change when it arises, and to create a feeling of *esprit de corps* within the organisation. If the book represents the 'state of the art' of corporate culture studies, then it is a state of the art based on a very narrow conceptualisation of the idea of culture. The degree to which norms, for example, are internalised and create integrated and stable structures is, first of all, an empirical question, not something to be assumed through theory. Culture, if it is to have any meaning, needs to be related to the total organisation, not regarded as phenomena solely vested in the hands of management. The idea that culture is the collective will of the organisation—its personality, an invisible force or the organisation's soul—is a metaphysical explanation of behaviour and events that are impossible to observe. Any theory which assumes that culture is the internalisation of dominant norms and values must also assume that all members must hold to the dominant value system or else be 'outside culture'. Of course, such a stance flies in the face of reality, particularly when we consider organisations where management tends to belong to one social class and workers to another. In such organisations, values, norms and social meanings are structured by 'class cultures' and are a constant potential source for dispute, with strikes only one example where such disputes become overt conflicts. For example, it would be difficult to explain the 1984 strike of the British coal miners either in terms of the collective will of the corporation or in terms of the internalisation of dominant norms and values. As will be discussed later, norms and values have as much potential for creating conflict within organisations as they do for creating social cohesion.

It should be noted that just because organisational theorists may have borrowed the concept of culture from a certain social anthropological tradition, it does not necessarily mean that organisational theorists use the concept of culture in exactly the same way as would social anthropologists. For example, while Radcliffe-Brown and other social anthropologists have treated culture as an integral feature of the structure and function of all societies—relating specific cultures to particular social outcomes—some organisational theorists have been inclined to treat culture as either exotic or 'irrational' behaviour (Kanter, 1977). More importantly, several studies of organisational culture have moved the concept of culture beyond that of a unifying and regulatory mechanism towards it being a form of social control created and manipulated by management. Baker (1980), for example, writes about 'managing organisational culture' and Allen and Kraft (1982) attempt to illustrate 'how to create the corporate culture you want and need'. Schein (1985:2) maintains that 'organisational cultures are created by leaders, and one of the most decisive functions of leadership may well be the creation, the management, and—if and when that may become necessary—the destruction of culture'. According to Schein (1985:2) 'we must recognise the centrality of this culture management function in the leadership concept'. [...]

It has often been that one of the crucial weaknesses of structural functional theory is its reliance on a biological metaphor (see, in particular, Nisbet, 1969). In accordance with the metaphor, the theory assumes that an organisation can be understood as either a huge organism or a 'superindividual'; hence, 'culture' is transferred from the individual actors who create and reproduce it to the organisation as a whole. Since it is the organic organisation that has 'culture', culture, including members' norms, values and beliefs, is necessarily a mechanism that creates organisational unity; the parts of a healthy organism do not work against themselves. [...]

The use of organic simile and the idea that culture can be regarded as the collective consciousness of the group are mostly derived from the theories of Durkheim. Although these theories remain in vogue, it is important to note past criticisms:

> The metaphysical concepts of a group mind, collective sensorium or consciousness are due to an apparent antinomy of sociological reality: the psychological nature of human culture on the one hand and on the other the fact that culture transcends the individual. The fallacious solution of this antinomy is the theory that human minds combine or integrate and form a superindividual and yet essentially spiritual being [...] Such concepts as

> consciousness of kind orthe inevitability of collective imitation, account for the psychological yet superindividual nature of social reality by introducing some theoretical metaphysical short cut. (Malinowski, 1930: 623)

In incorporating the idea of collective consciousness into that of organisational culture many theorists have failed to also incorporate the historical cricitisms attached to the original notion.

Individuals create and reproduce culture, but obviously they do not do so in a vacuum. The resources the individual has to draw upon in creating culture are not manufactured by the individual. Language is the classic example: no one person creates language, but we all use language creatively (Giddens, 1982). This point will be examined in more detail below.

The human relations school of 'scientific' management deserves special mention for it was the first body of theorists to explore informal social relations in organisations and to take the concept of organisational culture seriously (see Perrow, 1979 for a review of the history of the human relations school), but the human relations theorists have approached organisational culture mainly from a behaviourist-oriented psychological framework. The language used by human relations theorists is based on a medical/biological metaphor: they speak of healthy and unhealthy organisational culture or climate and talk about organisational hygiene. Human relations theorists regard culture as something which an organisation has and which can be manipulated to serve the ends of management. In summarising past research efforts of the human relations school, Gregory (1983:361) argues that the school's 'promanagement position resulted in biased research that studied the 'irrational' behaviour of lower ranking personnel and supported unquestioningly the "rational manager" model'. Moreover:

> The current corporate culture studies are not substantially different from earlier Human Relations research, in that the goal is still to illustrate the impact of 'irrational' human factors on 'rational' corporate objectives. 'Rational' corporate objectives correspond to management's goals for the organisation. Researchers in both areas sought to provide

> managers with tools to assess and control the organisational culture of their subordinates. (Gregory, 1983:361)

Despite such criticisms, practitioners, as well as academic researchers, have been intent upon discovering what creates 'healthy' and 'unhealthy' organisational culture. Managers of large corporations have come to think that economic success is somehow linked with the type of organisational culture or climate that they create. The idea of corporate culture has been pursued in such popular forms as *Business Week* 1980 and *Fortune Magazine* 1982. Ouchi's (1981) work, and the development of 'Theory Z' linking successful and unsuccessful organisational performance to the type of culture created by American and Japanese companies, has gained great popularity. Corporate managers seem to believe that a unifying organisational culture can be created and manipulated, and are prepared to pay good money to back their beliefs: 'the marketing of "corporate culture" is largely underway' (Smircich, 1983:346).

Those intent upon creating a 'healthy' and 'successful' corporate climate are often blind to 'what is' by their pursuit of 'what should be' (Gregory, 1983; Smircich, 1983; Allaire and Firsirotu, 1984). Corporate success, particularly economic success, is dependent far more upon external environmental influences and the vagaries of the market-place than on internal interpersonal dynamics. More importantly, the assumption that a corporate culture can be created so as to unite members for the effective and efficient attainment of corporate goals flies in the face of almost everyone's experience of organisational life. Organisations are often arenas for dispute and conflict, and one of the main items under dispute is often values. Organisations are not one homogeneous culture, but are 'multicultural', and culture can be a source of conflict (Gregory, 1983). Cultural conflict is most obvious in professional organisations—large teaching hospitals, research laboratories, tertiary education institutions. C.P. Snow's thesis of two cultures manifests itself month after month in every meeting of a university's academic board. Several studies have shown that academics may tend to give greater allegiance to their profession than to their college or university, which may produce conflict between the interest of the individual academic and the interests of those who manage the institution. Unity within organisational subcultures (academic departments, for example) can be a source of conflict as the various subcultures compete for both scarce resources prestige.

Nonetheless, human relations and related fields of study, and their preoccupation with the idea of a healthy or successful corporate culture, need to be taken seriously for two reasons. First, there are successful and not-so successful organisations, and there is something about the successful organisation that goes beyond explanations based on superior technology, efficient management and an advantageous position in the market-place. There is a certain 'feel' about the successful school, university or large corporation, and the phenomenon, whatever it is and whatever 'success' may mean, deserves investigation.

Second, while organisations may be regarded as forums for conflict and dispute, they also wield power in modern society through what Galbraith (1983) terms their ability to *condition* their own members and the public at large. Organisations have access to the three primary instruments of power: condign power (physical), compensatory power (economic) and conditioned power (belief). According to Galbraith, conditioned power is the most important in modern industrial society, and organisation is the locus of conditioned power. It is through 'persuasion, education, or the social commitment to what seems natural, proper or right' that the corporation, educational institution, church and the state 'cause the individual to submit to the will of another or of others' (Galbraith, 1983:23). Organisations may also enforce their will through the use of physical or economic power. In the past, the church was particularly prone to exercise its power through such means, but conditioned power is central 'to the functioning of the modern economy and polity, and in capitalist and socialist countries alike' (Galbraith, 1983:23). Thus, it is imperative that we understand the beliefs, symbols, myths, ideologies and folklores—the 'culture'—of the modern organisation as a form of social control. It is not a form of social control created and manipulated by management, but a process in which management, workers and the community at large participate alike.

Furthermore, Galbraith (1983) argues that there is a symmetric relationship between how power is exercised and how it is challenged: condign power is met with violence, compensatory power is met with the regulation of the market-place, and conditioned power is met with countervailing beliefs and ideologies. Consumer and environmental action groups represent a good example of a symmetric challenge to the conditioned power of modern corporations. In this respect, organisational culture is not a force for social integration, but a phenomenon likely to breed 'counter-cultures'.

An adequate theory of culture needs to be divorced from the direct interests of management and the naive assumption that a 'successful corporate culture' is either 'naturally good and stabilising' or can be 'consciously manipulated'. Just because group interaction within an organisation is based on norms and symbols, it does not necessarily follow that consensus and cohesion, based on shared and internalised value systems, are the result. Hopefully, the structural–functional theoretical assumptions on which the biomorphic, cohesive, integrative and stabilising characteristics of organisational studies of corporate culture rest have been adequately demonstrated and critiqued, and the need for a theory of culture that more adequately takes account of the contextual richness of social life within the organisation as a whole has been illustrated. Before suggesting alternative ways of viewing corporate culture, a few additional words need to be said about the manipulation of culture.

While it is maintained that culture *as a whole* cannot be consciously manipulated by management or any other group, culture is not necessarily static: cultures do change within organisations, and management does have more direct control than other organisational members over certain aspects of the corporate cultures, such as control over logos and officially stated missions and ethos. In this regard, some scholars have expressed concern that certain organisations can foster an allegiance to a corporate ethos that borders on religious fervour, while the ethos itself is of questionable social value (Turner, 1986). The way in which management attempts to intervene in the culture of an organisation should be a research priority, particularly in relation to the potential 'conditioned power' of organisation. However, empirically assessing the power and ability of management to intervene in the culture of an organisation and assuming through theory that management creates, changes and imposes 'culture' on a passive and uncritical membership—that management creates a cultural milieu in which rank-and-file staff are immersed and have no choice but to internalise its embedded norms and values—are quite separate considerations.

If culture emerges from the social interaction of all organisational members (as is argued here), then the way in which management may attempt to manipulate organisational symbols, myths, customs, etc., must be interpreted in relation to the *total* organisational culture of which management itself is only one part. Hitler did not create Nazi Germany by himself. It may be the case that some organisations are more prone to accept executive control, including control over organisational symbols and meanings, than are other organisations, but again, this is, first of all, an empirical question, not something that can be assumed through theory. Also, power, as Weber maintained, is exercised not merely through its acceptance by others, but rests on having the resources—which flow, at least in part, from one's position in the social structure—to impose one's will on others despite opposition.

While, in practice, questions of power, conflict and culture in the modern organisation cannot be divorced, the symbiotic relationship between the phenomena may be more adequately understood if a conceptual distinction is drawn between culture and social structure. We will now look at what consequences such a distinction may have for a theory of organisational or corporate culture.

Towards a Theory of Culture

While the idea of organisational culture has been approached in a variety of ways, the various theories, basically, fall into two camps or schools (Smircich, 1983). First, as was argued above, there are those who treat organisational culture as a variable: it is something that an organisation has (see Cummings and Schmidt, 1972; Schwartz and Davis, 1981; Deal and Kennedy, 1982; Peters and Waterman, 1982). Second, there is the view that 'culture is something an organisation is' (Smircich, 1983:347; and see Harris and Cronen, 1979; Weick, 1979; Morgan, 1980; Wacker, 1981). The second approach is much more closely aligned to the way in which anthropologists treat culture. Rather than regarding culture as something imported into an organisation from the broader society, or as something created by managementment, those theorists believe that culture is the product of negotiated and shared symbols and meanings; it emerges from social interaction. In this approach to culture, the researcher is not analysing some 'irrational' or exotlic aspect of organisational life. The interpretation of organisational culture must be deeply embedded in the contextual richness of the total social life of organisational members. Culture cannot be treated as being incidental, or outside of, the 'true purpose' of the organisation (Gregory, 1983).

Treating culture as emerging from social interaction—treating it as something that the organisation 'is', rather than treating it as a variable that can be manipulated by management—has obvious research implications. It also has political implications. If culture is regarded as embedded in social interaction, that is, as something that is socially produced and reproduced over time, influencing people's behaviour in relation to the use of language, technology, rules and laws, and knowledge and ideas (including ideas about legitimate authority and leadership), then it cannot be discovered or mechanically manipulated; it can only be described and interpreted. The researcher adopting the social emergent view of culture cannot suggest how it can be created or destroyed; the researcher can only attempt to record and examing how culture may be altered in the process of social reproduction. People do not just passively absorb meanings and symbols; they produce and reproduce culture, and in the process of reproducing it, they may transform it, the social emergent approach to culture also moves the researcher away from the political and ideological interests of management, towards those of the organisational community as a whole. [...]

For the purposes of analysis and interpretation, it seems necessary to distinguish between culture and social structure, but in so doing, two factors must be kept firmly in mind. First, culture and structure are two sides of the same coin they are parallel and complementary and constantly interacting with one another:

> One of the more useful ways—but far from the only one—of distinguishing between culture and social system is to see the former as an ordered system of meaning and of

> symbols, in terms of which social interaction takes place; and to see this latter as the pattern of social interaction itself. (Geertz, 1973:144)

Second, both culture and structure are abstractions, not tangible entities:

> The difference between the two concepts is not that one is an abstraction and the of the concerete, observable unit of behaviour, for both are abstractions of regularities from observations of actual behaviour, whether these regularities are implied and unconscious or explicit and verbalised. (Singer, 1968:533).

The task for the researcher in the field is not to observe culture or structure, but to observe the concrete behaviour of individual actors. Culture and social structure are not concrete entities; rather they are abstract concepts that are to be used to interpret behaviour. Geertz's (1973:5) definition of culture clearly focuses the attention of the researcher on concrete behaviour: 'Believing, with Max Weber, that man is an animal suspended in webs of significance he himself has spun, I take culture to be those webs, and the analysis of it to be therefore not an experimental science in search of law but an interpretive one in search of meaning.' [...]

The Dissection of Culture

[...] Symbol is the most inclusive of the various cultural derivatives, 'not only because language, ritual, and myth are forms of symbolism but because symbolic analysis is a form of reference, a style of analysis in its own right' (Pettigrew, 1979:575). Symbols are shared codes of meaning and include a variety of things—words, stories, icons, organisational logos or national flags—that provide 'meanings, evoke emotions, and impel men [and women] to action' (Cohen, 1974:23). Language is a representation, a symbol, of the real thing. Organisations may be distinguished by the language their members use: academics use jargon to mystify knowledge and computer programmers use a language that mystifies everyone but themselves. The guard tower is a symbol of both the concentration camp and the modern prison, impelling individuals to a form of negative action.

Religious icons may, on the one hand, unite the faithful, and on the other, lead them to scourge the infidel.

Organisation has itself been defined as being nothing more or less than patterns of symbolic discourse. Within the phenomenology, symbolic interactionism and ethnomethodology schools:

> organisations become *figments of participant's interpretation of their organisational experience;* they have no external reality but are merely social creations and construction *emerging* from actors making sense out of ongoing streams of actions and interactions. In what Burrell and Morgan (1979:260) call their *interpretive paradigm,* 'organisations simply do not exist'. (Allaire and Firsirotu, 1984:208)

This approach to organisational analysis is in danger of collapsing the social organisational and cultural components of social life into one unitary concept. As argued above, there is a need to maintain a conceptual distinction between culture and social structure, particularly for the purposes of investigating change and conflict. When the sociostructural pattern of human organisation is collapsed into being solely a pattern of symbolic discourse, 'the dynamic elements in social change which arise from the failure of cultural patterns to be perfectly congruent with forms of social organisation are largely incapable of formation' (Geertz, 1957:992)

An organisation is, of course, a structured association of individuals, and it is individuals who create meanings and symbols. Organisation cannot be reduced to the individual, for to do so misinterprets the significance, and the power, of organisation. MacIntyre puts the case in relation to the military organisation thus:

> You cannot characterise an army by referring to the soldiers who belong to it. For to do that you have to identify them as soliders; and to do that is already to bring in the concept of an army. For a soldier just is an individual who belongs to an army. Thus we see that the characterisation of individuals and of classes [or organisations] has to go together. Essentially these are not two separate tasks. (Quoted in Thompson, 1978:30)

Certainly, symbols are worthy of the researcher's attention. If the symbolic mode of interpretation is to consider the dynamics of change and conflict, then it seems that symbols need to be analysed in terms of a 'dialogue' between actor's sets of meanings and other social organisational aspects of the institution.

Closely related to the idea of culture as patterns of symbolic discourse is the notion of culture as ideational or cognitive systems, i.e. cultures seen as systems of knowledge (Keesing, 1974). One of the main proponents of this stance in anthropology is Goodenough:

> A society's culture consists of whatever it is one has to know or believe in order to operate in a manner acceptable to its members. Culture is not a material phenomenon; it does not consist of things, people, behaviour, or emotions. It is rather an organisation of these things. It is the form of things that people have in mind, their models for perceiving, relating, and otherwise interpreting them. (Quoted in Keesing, 1974:77)

Obviously, men and women must share some knwoledge in common in order to act in concert: organised work would be impossible if people did not share some meanings, knowledge systems and symbols. 'Most occupations...operate on the premise that the people who work in them know certain procedures and certain ways of thinking about and responding to typical situations and problems' (Becker, 1982:522). However, like symbolic interactionism, the ideational or cognitive theory of organisational culture fails when it is elevated to a universal theory that attempts to explain all social organisational phenomena. 'Analyses of cultures as cognitive systems have not progressed very far beyond a mapping of limited and neatly bonded semantic domains' (Keesing, 1974:78). Organisational culture is too rich and diverse to be amenable to a comprehensive interpretation through ideational codes, however sophisticated their elaboration.

However, the investigation of cognitive systems can be a powerful analytical tool so long as the interpretation of ideas and knowledge is related to, but kept separate from, social structural issues. It is here that the concept of ideology may play an important role. Ideology is not only 'a set of beliefs about the social world and how it operates', but also contains ethical statements 'about the rightness of certain social arrangements' (Wilson, 1973:91). An ideology may be congruent with the social structure, or it may be expressly divergent from the pattern of social interaction within the organisation. Also, an organisation may contain a number of ideologies, with ideological groupings in competition with one another over such issues as power and legitimate authority. These are, of course, empirical questions that can be answered only through research.

Contrary to the popular lay definition, myth is not regarded by anthropologists as an erroneous story. Rather, 'a myth is a narrative of events; the narrative has a sacred quality; the sacred communication is made in symbolic form; at least some of the events and objects which occur in the myth neither occur nor exist in the world other than that of myth itself; and the narrative refers in dramatic form to origins or transformations' (Cohen, 1969:337). Organisational myths or stories certainly do not constitute all that is 'cultural' is an organisation, but the interprelation of organisation members' myths and folklores is one angle of attack on the problem of organisational culture that has proved to be fruitful. Creation myths are usually thought of as something belonging to traditional societies, but members of modern organisations also have their stories about how the organisation came into being and how it developed over time. Clark terms such folk stories or myths 'organisational sagas':

> Saga...has come to mean a narrative of heroic exploits, of a unique development that has deeply stirred the emotions of participants and descendants. Thus, a saga is not simply a story but a story that at some time has had a particular base of believers. (Clark, 1972:178-9)

The notion of an organisational saga is a useful theoretical tool for the study of certain aspects of symbolic behaviour. As a concept it gives importance to publicly expressed stories about group uniqueness; it is an explanation of what makes an organisation unique and distinctive in the eyes of its members. In theory, these stories or 'folk histories' may function as symbolic justifications for member's actions in concrete situations.

Martin *et al.* (1983:439), while recognising the emphasis on uniqueness in organisational stories and sagas, maintain that there are also 'similarities in content and structure' in all such stories: 'a culture's claim to uniqueness is expressed through cultural manifestations that are not in fact unique. This is the uniqueness paradox.' Anthropologists, such as Malinowski, Levi-Strauss, and others, have also looked at the creation myths of different traditional societies in order to discover similarities in content and structure.

It also needs to be recognised that myths, folklores and sagas may be a source of conflict, particularly in the context of rapid social change. There is evidence to suggest that at least one organisation's saga, while appropriate to the development of the institution during a particular historical period, became quite inappropriate and caused disunity, following dramatic changes in the institution's external political environment (Meek, 1982). In another study (Meek, 1984), it was argued that the organisation had developed two sets of shared beliefs and ideologies that were in competition with one another: a saga and a counter-saga.

All organisations have forms of ritualised behaviour. A university, for example, would not be a university without the ritual and symbols that surround such events as graduation ceremonies and inaugural lectures. The ritual is as old as the idea of the university itself. At graduation, academics and graduands clothe themselves in medieval garb and speak in foreign tongues—Latin. The procession preceding an inaugural lecture is led by the bearer of arms carrying a mace. Except for historians, most members of the university organisation have long forgotten the origin and function of such cultural artifacts as the academic gown and mace, but they all know that these artifacts symbolise the university, and they share a feeling of belonging to an academic community whenever the artifacts are displayed and the ritual is performed.

According to Benedict (1934:396), ritual simply is the 'prescribed formal behaviour for occasions not given over to technological routine'. This definition is attractive in its simplicity, although it leaves the question of how rituals are to be interpreted unanswered. Anthropologists (Beattie, 1966) and organisational theorists (Pettigrew, 1979) often maintain that what is important is what rituals 'say' not what they 'do'. In this sense, Harrison (1951) maintained that 'ritual is a dramatisation of myth'.

However, Leach (1968:524) argues that 'ritual may "do things" as well as "say things". The most obvious examples are healing rituals which form a vast class and have a world-wide distribution.' Ritualised physical exercise in Japanese industries is both an expression of corporate allegiance and a mechanism for maintaining the health of the workforce.

It is often assumed that rituals legitimise established authority, and 'provide a shared experience of belonging and express and reinforce what is valued' (Pettigrew, 1979:576). However, as Gluckman (1962) has shown, 'rituals of rebellion' may have the opposite function: they allow people to act out hostilities that may not be expressed in normal everyday social relations.

The interpretation of ritual is just as complicated as any other aspect of cultural behaviour. However, research into the ritualisation of behaviour should not assume from the outset that ritual expresses and sanctifies the established social order. It may do this, but ritual may also be a mechanism for maintaining one group in power despite the will of others, or it may be a dramatised expression of rebellion of one group against others. Once again, these are empirical questions, not something that can be assumed through theory.

Summary

There has been a tendency for some researches to treat organisational culture as a 'variable' that can be controlled and manipulated like any other organisational variable. Culture *as a whole* cannot be manipulated, turned on and off, although it needs to be recognised that some are in a better position than others to attempt to intentionally influence aspects of it. The tendency to assume otherwise results, at least in part, from the selective way in which the concept of culture has been borrowed from anthropology and sociology. The basis of the argument presented in this chapter is that culture should be regarded as something that an organisation 'is', not as something that an organisation 'has': it is not an independent variable, nor can it be created, discovered or destroyed by the whims of management. Nonetheless, it seems necessary for the purposes of the interpretation of actors' behaviour, that a conceptual distinction be made between 'culture' and 'social structure'. It must be kept in mind, though, that both culture and structure are abstractions, and have use only in relation to the interpretation of observed concrete behaviour. This chapter, however, does not advance any one elaborats or steadfast theoretical model of cultural interpretation; for 'it is going to take more than one kind of theoretical model to do justice to the variety, complexity, and richness of human culture' (Singer, 1968:541).

7

Executive Development

Twenty years ago, at the end of the first week of the first Dartmouth Institute, a mover and shaker among international bankers raised his hand and asked, 'what in hell are we doing here?' Courses in the humanities have long been offered in executive development programs, but their content and methodology can seem anomalous because they do not contain a rationale for immediate practical application. In this paper I will try to frame an answer to the banker's question by showing that the humanities offer unique and intelligible beenefits to the practice of management. The special province of the humanities is the study of *values* in their most basic and potent forms, and such study has an important relevance to the contemporary exercise of executive responsibility.

In executive education, every program, seminar, of course must offer a worthwhile approach to the art and science of management. Just as there are good reasons for courses in marketing or finance, reasons that derive from the actual needs of executives in their professional lives, so there are good reasons for courses in the liberal arts; they also meet practical needs. But the way in which liberal arts courses do this is very different from that of marketing and finance courses. This difference causes much confusion, especially in the relatively recent educational undertaking called executive development.

Built into most courses in professional schools, whether they are schools of business, medicine, law, or even graduate schools in the humanities, is the rationale for the existence of the course itself. Courses in pathology, torts, or finance teach students how to do something, how to reach a practical end, and they constantly affirm their relation to that goal. Most executive development courses also follow this pattern. But for executives (or doctors or lawyers) who suddenly find themselves in a liberal arts course reading Sophocles or Shakespeare, the rationale is not at all apparent.

There is a good reason for this. Assigning liberal arts courses a practical, immediate end would undermine their real value. This paradox lies at the heart of all higher learning: as soon as you give it an objective, a functionally defined goal, it ceases to produce the widely functional definitions that are its raison d'etre. For example, a course that proposes to teach students to think philosophically is a contradiction in terms: one cannot think philosophically by aiming at a single goal (even if that goal is to think philosophically). Such absurd courses do in fact exist, but their claims are misleading. The power of authentic liberal arts courses is always latent, always potential. Their power can only be released in and through the minds of the individual participants. No professor can tell an executive when and how the material and methods of thought will prove their value, will become 'useful'. The liberal arts teacher knows that Sophocles and Shakespeare (themselves great students of the art and science of management) will help in the 'real world', but their concrete application by any individual executive is unknown and may remain so. Relativity Theory or Cubism may teach an executive the breakthrough skill of counterintuitive thinking, but the crucial moment when this 'pays off' cannot be predicted.

Thus the material and methods of liberal arts courses must by nature be widely diffusive and highly personal in order to function properly in the practical, professional sphere as well as in personal life. On the one hand, the lack of a single aim or result obscures the value of the liberal arts. But on the other hand, the essentially diffusive and personal quality of application gives the liberal arts course its extraordinary depth, flexibility, and power. And these qualities are precisely the ones that executives who take and evaluate such courses consistently appreciate.

If liberal arts courses have a tendency to rise above the bottom line it is not because their proponents are superior to practical and professional considerations. For grudging competitiveness and unyielding professional ambition I will match liberal arts professors against any other group worldwide. The fact is that liberal arts courses *must* rise above the bottom line if they are to offer their distinctive value. To maintain the intimacy and flexibility from which they draw their power, they must resist any accounting that ties them to a single definition of intellectual profit.

The Study of Values

I am defending the humanities here for two reasons. First, they are my primary field of specialisation, and second, they are the field most vulnerable to charges of irrelevance and impracticality. Most educated people recognise the importance of the natural sciences (at least in their technological applications) in our economic and political life. Most see the social sciences as usefully concerned with the continued functioning of our pluralistic democracy. If I can make a case for the humanities, my reasoning goes, then by extension I can make a case for the more obviously useful sciences and social sciences. Beyond this I have a secret and probably unprovable conviction that the study of the humanities at the highest level actually comprehends and prefigures study in the natural and social sciences. Or—to put it less imperialistically—real scientific knowledge and discovery is humanistic knowledge and discovery (I even know a few scientists who agree with this).

So what do the humanities do that the other areas of study and thought don't do? Humanities courses try to answer questions like, 'What in hell are we doing here?' When Shakespeare's Hamlet asks his well-known question, 'To be or not to be?' we understand it in a large, philosophical context. We do not ask him, 'To be or not to be *what?*' We allow for the range of his inquiry. We allow him to ask about the fundamental value of being alive. Hamlet goes on to conclude that there is no available practical answer: the human condition denies us the information to reach a bottom-line answer about the value of being. He concludes that we lack the resources to come to a conclusion—and, as he is tragically aware, the effect is to inhibit us from taking the gratifying practical action (killing the king). Does this mean that Hamlet's inquiry is without meaning? As with many executive decisions, Hamlet's restraint is a matter of personal judgment.

Hamlet's question—like the question 'What in hell are we doing here?'—is not about fact. No empirical conclusion or statistical summary will give the answer. These are questions about values, and the only division of learning that studies the nature of values is the humanities. I do not mean that other branches of learning do not *work with* values. Natural science is deeply committed to such values as accuracy and verification. The social sciences perpetually allude to values (liberty, equàlity, solidarity, free market economy, and so forth). But neither really asks what values are and how human beings apply them when they make choices and act. It is the humanities that tell us how people deal with what they most deeply feel and believe in their most intense expressions—in their art and science, in their ethical choices and moral lives. Such values are often quite different from the abstractions affirmed in political speeches and manifestos.

The word 'values' has many meanings. A true value may or may not be ethically positive. For example, many political officeholders use the phrase 'family values', mushy formulation aimed to strike a positive chord in voters. No doubt many of these politicians are sincere. But the phrase they choose to use is vague—'family values.' Some officeholders who don't care at all about children or the family (to judge from their voting records) use these words. Similarly, many of the same people give the impression that they are talking about values when they affirm their support for 'the American way of life.' This formulation suggests a kind of national stew of values that can be stirred in various ways to engage the atention of American voters, and no doubt the stew consists of a number of common ingredients that give off an aroma recognisable by a majority of us.

But students of the humanities pursue something more specific and more primary than these vague slogans. Someone trained in the study of language—that is, someone trained in the basic technology of the humanities—will look at the two phrases 'family values' and 'The American way of life' and recognise a similarity in their mode of expression. Deep down, beneath the putative affirmations, the words contain an element in common, an element that I call a 'value.' And that value is the *vagueness* itself. The phrases 'family values' and 'the American way of life' don't say anything explicit about vagueness, but they are characterised by and validate vagueness. The student of language and expression sees that our political leaders like such phrases not because they are devoted to family and country (they may or may not be) but because they like vague phrases that keep them out of trouble with voters. In a highly pluralistic society vagueness is a proven value when you run for office. The more you can disguise the actual ingredients of your candidacy, the fewer groups you will alienate. Many voters seem to sense and approve of this—as they approved in such numbers of President Regan's soothing paternal generalisations. So an underlying *value* in such appeals, one that is not explicit but that is nevertheless closer to the true agendas of their usage than the values explicitly affirmed (whatever these may be), is their indefiniteness. The agenda for the politicians is to get elected, and the agenda for the voters is to elect somebody whose position does not separate them from each other by pressing specifics. Such agendas may be as important in American life as family or national identity. In this way indefiniteness, vagueness, ro even evasiveness may be a *value* whether or not the person who holds it perceives or acknowledges it as such. Finally, we need to remember that we got to this conclusion by looking at the *language* of the politicians, their *habit of expression*. That is we employed a distinctly humanistic mode of analysis. In this kind of analysis, values are the most primitive and primary dispositions, the most elemental social coordinates, the ultimate constituents of our actions.

Let me offer a somewhat fancier example of a distinctively humanities-based analysis. Let's take two primary values of postmodern literature (cutting-edge fiction roughly since World War II): *play* and *reflexivity*. The work of postmodern writers—Borges, Cortázar, Robbe-Grillet, Hawkes, for example—validates the ideas of *play* (actions and patterns that have immediate or formal rather than utilitarian value) and *reflexivity* (the idea that meaning is generated within closed systems, and not in relation to any external 'reality'—a derogated concept in postmodernism). Thus a postmodern film or novel may show the same events happening over and over again (as in the works of Robbe-Grillet) with only slight but troubling and possibly sinister variations. The reader notices these variations and by a process of comparison arrives at the understanding that these are patterns whose importance derives only from their relation (play) to each other; there is no one 'true' (privileged) version of the events. Or the reader may observe a protagonist working toward a solution to a mystery (as in stories by Borges and Cortázar) only to realise that the mystery offers no 'solution' in the 'real', external world (what world is that?) but contains meaning exclusively within the self-referential framework of the work of fiction. Thus in postmodern literature there is the latent but finally obvious equation of fiction with reality and of reality with fiction. This is a logical consequence of making play and reflexivity primary values

It is true that cutting-edge fiction immediately affects quite limited numbers of people, and that only a few of these are corporate executives (although more than most liberal arts professors think). But fortunately for specialists in the humanities, the culture's dominant values are not field-specific. We can, for example, see the same tendencies surfacing in the media (as might be expected, there's a lag between avant-garde fiction and journalism). Until quite recently, the news on television or in the daily paper presented itself as an account of reality, a description of what was going on in the world. Of course many newspeople were openly critical or cynical about the degree of accuracy in news reports, but they still believed that the news had some connection with a real world independent of our perception of it. Many of us can remember Walter Cronkite ending his newscast every weekday with the endearing and somehow reassuring phrase, 'And that's the way it is...' But recent years have seen a shift away from actual events and toward the *perception* of actual events. Dan Rather, Peter Jennings, and the others show less concern with actuall U.S. policy and practice than with how people *judge* our policy and practice. The question is not so often what President Bush's stand on taxes really is but on how his stand is perceived by the person in the street, by rightwing Republicans, and so on. We appear to care less about the actual effects of our support of, say, Israel, than about how US voters *feel about* our support of Israel. In other words, the media shows a growing tendency to concern itself not with trying to describe actualities but with trying to describe the attitudes of the media audience. News organisations commonly conduct media polls (such as those by CBS/*New*

York Times and NBC/*Wall Street Journal*) and report the results (which measure perceptions and attitudes) as *news*. Not only is the media in the business of describing pereptions, it is in the business of turning these descriptions into news itself. The whole industry increasingly seems to consist of the media's continuous self-reflection, its *play of reflexivity*. So that even devoted students of postmodernism long for the return of the media to its former mission of pretending to report real events from a real world. But reeality—as students of postmodern literature know well and as newspeople seem at least to intuit—is fading as a *value*.

Postmodern Money

Well, so what? What does all this have to do with the price of junk bonds (as my banker friend might well ask)? I answer that if certain values turn up in postmodern literature and the news media, they may very well turn up in contemporary finance, in what I'll call 'postmodern money'. What follows represents a deliberately high-risk investment in the methods of value analysis. As always, it is the reader (the investor) who will judge whether it performs well.

Widely evident in financial scandals of the last few years is an increasing departure from the investment community's connection with the productive energy of the economy. This connection was its link to the concrete (real) world of goods and services and was generally thought to justify speculation in the 'free' market. Such an ethos of work-ingenuity-risk used to constitute 'the American way of life.' Money (I was taught in my high school civics course) was invested in the production of goods and services, especially goods. Capital financed industry, which produced goods. Goods were freely traded, and the result was increasing national wealth. My civics teacher, dear old Adam Smith, told us that the production and exchange of goods eventually produced more capital; this capital could be reinvested; and the 'invisible hand' of free trade would see that all parties prospered.

Boy, have times changed! Postmodern investment couldn't care less what was actually being produced or traded. What turned out to be important was not building an industry but something much more simple: numbers. What counts in postmodern money is how much (or more accurately how *many*) you have. We don't care if it's airlines or biscuits. We can reduce it to a common point system (the points in this high scoring game are called dollars) and tell who's won. It's not the 'real world' (as in airplanes and passengers, farmers and grain supplies, books and readers) but the *game* that counts. One doesn't invest in an industry; one invests in an *opportunity*. One is not interested in producing *things:* that's not what *players* do because that's not how you *win*.

To the extent that this cartoon of postmodern money has validity, many members of the financial community deplore it. Unfortunately, however, the cartoon is accurate enough to describe the values (in our precise sense of the word) of a number of highflyers. I'm speaking of the bizarre collection of crooks and clowns who engineered the insider trading and S&L scandals. These people got absorbed in the game. They adopted the postmodern value of *play* with one important element left out. They became so self-referential, so solipsistically *reflexive*, that they lost sight of another key postmodern perception: that the absence of a privileged reality means that they didn't have it either. They believed their game comprehended all other games. In the end they seemed to be aware only of each other, the knowing few, the few with the privileged information. In the end they made up their own ethics. But—to keep the game metaphor, itself a value in our sense—the board was bigger than they thought. There turned out to be other agendas, competing interests, the requisite sucker majority—so some highflyers got caught. The comments of such players, many of them made in court, when nalysed to separate the euphemisms from the operative values, reveal a breathtaking lack of any sense of responsibility to the people defrauded and injured by their actions. And still less evident is any awareness of obligation to the systems (free enterprise capitalism, basic business ethics) to which they owe their wealth and power, the context of their *opportunities*.

Values like play and reflexivity in themselves are neither good nor bad. No doubt every period and culture contains its own highflyers and its own values whose misuse can sweep them away. But my point concerns what I see as a remarkable affinity between what has been going on in contemporary cutting edge fiction, in the media, and in financial practice. We can see this affinity in the film *Wall Street,* which, though probably exaggerated, effectively summarises the ethos of the hostile takeover. Here Michael Douglas plays the highflyer: Gekko is a genius not only at making the right deal at the right time but—like some of his prototypes in 'real' life—also brilliant at advocating his own methods. In one scene he goes before a meeting of shareholders and defends his tactics as good for the company and the economy. At the conclusion of his forceful speech the shareholders (and some members of the movie audience) applaud him. But later on he tells his young protégé that his words are merely moves in the game, that they have no reference to anything outside the game (such as the employees of an airline he has acquired). In so doing he offers a postmodern definition of reality. He says that he makes the news, that he is the news, that the news is whatever he says it is. Dealing as he does with the *perception* of value (the airline is worth whatever people think it is worth) he approaches *perception* directly. He bypasses the airline as a producer of valuable services. What might formerly have been thought of as the 'real' condition or value of the airline (its relation to employees, passengers, suppliers, assets, and the national transportation network), pales into irrelevance (becomes *unreal*) when compared to the value (in dollars, the points in the game) of the perceptions. Gekko sees himself as nothing less than the *creator* of his reality. He thus assumes an incomplete but authentically postmodern ethical posture. When he loses it's because he has mistaken his own game for the only game. In other words, he fails because he's not postmodern all the way, but (like the other criminal highflyers he's meant to stand for) gets trapped in his own solipsism, the victim of a primitive regression. He becomes a lizard, a gecko.

If I had space to present all the relevant material I have in hand (a lot), could I prove these connections between avant-garde literature, news media, and junk bonds? Certainly not: you don't *prove* values. But this does not mean that my evidence is 'soft', as is so often charged of the means by which we reach conclusions in the humanities. The materials I work with—words, events, values—are in many ways as hard and concrete in their identity, in their definition, as the empirical verification or statistical evidence of the natural and social sciences, or indeed of practical economics. If we want to compare the 'hardness' of our data (observe that in our information ethic, hardness is a positive value!), I'll put any text in my courses up against the annual report of any large corporation, and indeed against most analyses and reports that drive corporate policy. What I can't do (because the pedagogic technology of my discipline precludes it) is to forecast how, for example, my analysis of postmodern money might affect a particular executive's policy making. I can't do that because that action will take place in the executive's mind. But if I am correct in arguing that recent financial scandals represent not just the excesses of a few misguided spirits but instead the misapplication of widely shared changes in the general culture's value structure, then this argument might well affect the policy of government agencies and corporations. The important question becomes not whether I can 'prove' that my anslysis is correct but whether it might help executives to have more contact with this kind of thinking. Do policy makers need to know this? Do policy makers who can think humanistically (as well as economically and technologically) have a better chance of making wise decisions?

Ethics Anyone?

But (I can hear people asking) am I not really talking about *ethics?* Does not the real solution to the financial scandals lie much more simply in teaching business school graduate students courses in ethics, with maybe a refresher course for middle management? If the crooks and clowns of the S&L disaster had only had a good, solid course in ethics, starting, say, with Aristotle and moving up through Kant and on to current methods of evaluating stakeholder interests, wouldn't they have shunned the fraud that will cost taxpayers so dearly? It would, as Hemingway said in another context, be pretty to think so.

And some people do seem to think so, or at least to believe that certain adjustments to the business school curriculum may provide the answers. In a recent *New York Times* interview of three business school deans, Meyer Feldberg of Columbia asks, 'What is the correct mechanism for introducing morality and ethics into our curriculum, not just at the beginning but all the way through?' Latter in the interview, Dean Rosenblum of Darden offers this hypothesis: 'We have concluded that ethics is a discipline much like marketing, or any other discipline...We've decided to have a required course in ethics. But not a course that says this is right and that is wrong.' Dean Jacobs of the Kellogg Graduate School of Management argues, 'It is an irony that it was the scandals on Wall Street that caused us to be so concerned about the teaching [of] ethics on campus. But the scandals had nothing to do with ethics. They were simply against the law and that's different.'

Before I venture to disagree with so much prestige and power I want to say exactly where I stand on the teaching of ethics. Ethics is a well-established branch of philosophy, a discipline in the division of the humanities. As a humanities professor I regularly help to teach senior executive seminars in business ethics. I not only believe in the value of such seminars but enjoy some of the more rewarding moments of my professional life in helping to design and conduct them. But I don't believe they really produce ethical professionals. However able Columbia's business teachers may be, morality and ethics cannot be introduced by a 'mechanism', curricular or otherwise. I can easily imagine that if Darden's faculty has concluded that 'ethics is a discipline much like marketing', they don't talk much about 'this is right and that is wrong.' Finally, I believe that Dean Jacobs must have been misquoted when the Times has him saying that 'the scandals had nothing to do with ethics.' Even if mat were credible, ethics has everything to do with the scandals—but not the ethics of a curricular 'mechanism', not the ethics that is a discipline 'much like marketing.' What is being marketed here is not ethics, but business schools. This is not disingenuous of these deans. On the contrary, they are merely (and maybe a little casually) voicing a widespread assumption of US education: that if you find the right pedagogic technology you can teach anything. If only Iwan and Michael had heard my lecture on postmodern money!

But if ethics courses don't produce ethical executives then why offer courses or take seminars in business ethics? My answer is that ethics is valuable in the same way that other courses in the humanities are valuable, as a way of thinking about values. Ethics deals more directly with the process of moral choice than other courses, and it can offer methods for making such choices. But by itself it cannot teach anyone to make morally sound or ethically defensible decisions. Ethically defensible decisions are made by people who are morally fit, who have regularly practiced making ethically defensible decisions. When the fire starts, when the deal goes down, when pressure is on to bend the rules, nobody takes an ethics course. Executives act. That is why they are called *executives.* And only executives who have practiced thinking about values, who understand the full range of options, and who are not driven by cultural pressures (values) of which they are unconscious will make fully informed decisions.

I say 'fully informed' rather than 'morally right' because I know that it is possible for very alert people to make ethically indefensible decisions. They do it all the time. From the standpoint of ethics, many people who make such decisions know what they are doing and choose to go forward. They do this for the elementary reason that they want something and are willing to take unethical action in order to get it. When these unethical actions are also against the law, as of course a great many of them are, then we call these people criminals. Breaking the law *always* raises ethical issues though it may in specific cases be ethically defensible. The action I choose to take depends on the values I hold and the clarity of my conscious relation to them. To the extent that I know myself, I believe that I would not break the law to take unfair advantage of other traders in the marketplace, but I can imagine circumstances in which I would choose to break the law (to protect myself or someone I love from permanent harm, for example).

What one chooses to do depends in the end on the unimaginably complicated interaction of value structures at play inside the mind with the currents of multiple influence fromt he surrounding world. This process is so intimate, complex, and subtle that we have no adequate method for analysing it or predicting its effects. Thus, courses in ethics may suggest principles for decision making and methods for employing them (which of course are themselves value laden); they can clarify motives and possible consequences; they can offer a kind of moral aerobics to start us thinking about values. But they can never dictate action. Ethics courses, like other courses in the humanities, must teach *about* values but they can never 'teach values.' Still, what they do is enough. As I have been arguing all along, learning *about* values is an important value—especially for executives.

Courses in the liberal arts can never pretend to produce better people. This is because the liberal arts, in contrast to certain religious and political systems, don't claim to know what better is. We can deseribe and sometimes analyze; we don't prescribe and dictate. For us, the moral and ethical life provides an infinite source of professional interest but not of professional judgment. A student of values must always proceed warily because the relation of values to choice and action, especially what we call ethical choice and action, remains perpetually mysterious. But a student of the liberal arts will never be driven as blindly as others by the pressures of unperceived or undigested values. A true student of values may lose in the game of points, but not the way the Gekkos lose: from imagining themselves as the masters rather than as the actors in the play. Nobody *masters* values.

Captain Vere's Disease

But most managers are not Gekkos; most executives are not financial highflyers. I want to provide an example of humanistic thinking of relevance to the broad spectrum of readers. And here I can choose from a large range of possibilities, but one that fits my remaining space lies in Herman Melville's great story 'Billy Budd, Sailor.' Many readers will remember it from college courses and others will have come upon it again in executive development programs, where it is widely used. The dramatic center of the tale lies in the conflict between Captain Vere's belief in Billy's cosmic innocence and what Vere sees as the military necessity for hanging him. Billy, an image of youthful beauty and strength, is accused by a diabolical petty officer of treason. Because a speech impediment prevents him from declaring his innocence, Billy expresses his indignation in a lethal blow, which Vere witnesses. At this historical moment, Britain is at war with revolutionary France and the British navy has just experienced a serious mutiny. Vere decides that for the good of the navy and the nation he must apply the letter of the Mutiny Act. It is he who guides his handpicked drumhead court to the verdict. Melville makes it clear that throughout all this Vere feels nothing less than a paternal affection for Billy Budd and that Billy's execution is as much a 'crucifixion' of the captain himself as of the sailor. Billy's last words are 'God bless Captain Vere?'

In Captain Vere and his decision many executives see themselves and some of their decisions – on a more modest dramatic scale, of course. Nevertheless, in years of discussing this story with them I have rarely found one who would wholeheartedly support Vere's action. I find that for the sake of the discussion, *I* am the one who must make the case for the captain: that his authority and the order dependent on it were more important than the life of a single seaman, that his corporate responsibilities came first, and so on. Executives see clearly that Melville has placed Vere in a lose/lose situation: if he finds Billy innocent then he risks losing military discipline at the moment he, and Britain, need it most; but if he executes Billy he destroys something in himself and outrages higher principles of justice. It is not the toughness of his decision that bothers these readers. Most of them see the necessity for that. It is the premise of absolute alternatives, the absolutism in Vere's value structure, that offends them.

Most executives want to find a middle way; they are attracted to a compromise that Melville himself placed in the story as an ethical way out. This would be to isolate Billy until he could be handed over to the admiral (some day's sail distant). Vere rejects this on the grounds that it still constitutes an unacceptable risk to discipline in wartime, but his inferiors consider it the natural thing to do. Gradually the story permits readers to see that Vere's world contains several possible actions (ethical choices) that he could properly and legitimately take. He chooses the one most painful for Billy, for Billy's shipmates, and for himself. Was his decision the most efficient one from a military standpoint? There is no way of knowing (though Melville hints that the execution actually *unsettles* the crew). Ethically it can be defended, but only on rigid and disputable utilitarian grounds. And yet, despite the fact that most executives believe they would not have made his decision, there is a widespread consensus that Vere represents a condition very common among them. Executives generally agree that there is a level – an emotional level, perhaps – where Vere represents them. When I ask, for example, whether Vere's love for Billy makes it more or less likely that he will execute him, everybody agrees that his love for Billy makes it *more* likely.

I'm sorry to say that I, too, understand this. Perhaps I'm a closet executive and therefore see the necessity to execute. However I may disapprove of Vere's decision, however I may find it obsessive, I know intuitively why he takes it. Or, to put this in the context of my discussion, I see that Captain Vere embodies one of my cherished *values* – and this value is one that I share with all serious executives. It's a tendency to do more than is necessary, to stay later at work, to drive harder, to internalise the rules for success, to tighten them, to make them more austere than the context requires. I call this 'going *beyond* the book', in contrast to going by the book. To go beyond the book is to take the job description and then elevate it to a religion. This is not the same as being a workaholic. Presumably workaholics work addictively because they like it better than anything else. But Captain Vere's disease has us going *against* what we love and what we like. In this ethos, you know you are fulfilling your responsibilities when you are feeling pain. The Captain Veres of this world know that executing Billy (which of course stands for taking the action we find most distasteful) is right because it's the decision that hurts the most. Pain becomes a positive value.

All this might be ironically amusing if it were not so costly and so common. The most widespread executive problem in 1990, according to my humanistic calculation, was not ethical ignorance or moral laxity (though these weaknesses continued to attract attention). The chief problem for most executives that comes to light in my courses is that they have not taken the time or have not found the techniques to reconcile the values of their professional context with the values of their personal and private sphere. This is a loss. The professional ethos would benefit enormously from a massive injection of the kinds of values that most executives feel able to acknowledge only in a domestic context – their affective, emotional lives. In this regard, the workplace is said to be progressing, but in practice it shows itself liable to massive regressions. As women and minorities especially know, it is still usually a mistake to show your true feelings at the office. Discipline must be maintained.

The value disorder that Melville diagnosed in Captain Vere over a hundred years ago pursues us still. What is the cure? Again, this is the *application* of our analysis and as we know by now that always takes place in the minds of individuals. But in a general way we could say that Vere would have benefited from greater latitude in his thinking, a latitude that would allow for a direct connection with his emotional life. Instead of confining his consideration of the difficult situation before him to the letter of the Mutiny Act, he would have done well to open the doors of his mind to a wider range of influences. He represents the pitiful but familiar spectacle of an executive actually *narrowing* the range of his options. Executives often describe this as a failure of nerve. At his moral core the hero is a coward. Despite the fact that his subordinates suggest to him other sources of value—religion, civil law, natural law, natural pity—he goes at first by the book and then beyond the book of discipline. In the end his supreme value is airless, dissociated, pointless. What, we ask, is he fighting for? What is his business?

Who Needs It?

It should be clear by now that I believe the humanities, and by extension the liberal arts, to be essential to serious executive education. And in order to deliver their special benefits, liberal arts courses must remain free from the constraint of predefined practical objectives. But because their overall purpose is to provide methods of thought and substantive content that will help executives be better executives, these courses must be designed with them in mind. Courses developed for undergraduates, for graduate students in professional schools, or simply for adults who want to continue their liberal arts education, however excellent in themselves, are not sufficiently focused on executive concerns. Humanities courses designed specifically for executives development deal with values central to the practice of management. They treat such resonant themes as the exercise of power and its correlative responsibilities, or the nature of authority, its sources, archetypes, and embodiments. The challenge to executives lies in acknowledging the substance of humanistic thinking and practicing its techniques; the challenge to educators is to focus that thinking on areas of executive experience.

Provided these conditions are met, the returns can be considerable. They are suggested, I hope, in my examples of 'postmodern money' and 'Captain Vere's disease', but I owe the following list of benefits largely to appraisals from executive participants themselves. They have found:

- a widening of the perceived range of options and choices, both in the culture at large and in their relation to it;
- increased awareness of the integrity or unity of their experience and of connections between experiences in areas too often kept separate (e.g., personal-professional; aesthetic-technical);
- a consciousness of values otherwise latent and unperceived, in the general culture and in themselves;
- an increased perception of social and cultural direction or drift and an awareness of what is happening in worlds outside their own professions;
- increased ethical awareness (though not necessarily moral improvement) gained from practice in thinking about values and choices; and
- an opportunity to exercise influence or control in matters where such opportunity would previously have gone unperceived.

I think that such benefits justify the presence of the humanities in executive education. It is true that the questions we began with persist: How do these enlargements translate into better figures on the bottom line? What are we doing here? But now I can say with assurance that such questions, in order to contain value, must remain open.

8

Prescriptions for Success

There is no question that high-technology industries and the professional and high-tech work force are vital to the economic health and prosperity of the United States. The rapid development of high-tech industries and the subsequent demand for highly skilled scientists, engineers, and other technologically sophisticated secialists suggest that the third industrial revolution has now begun. The agents of change include the microprocessor, CAD/CAM, lasers, biogenetics, and a host of other new technologies (Finkelstein and Newman 1984).

At the core of these new technologies are the professionals and high-tech workers who research and develop the innovations that engineer change. This book has been concerned with the extent to which professional and high-tech workers are systematically different from nonprofessional workers. These differences demand innovative approaches to the management of human resources in high-tech industries. In turn, these innovative approaches to human-resource management are affected by the fact that high-tech firms operate within dynamic or "high velocity" environments (Bourgeois and Eisenhardt 1987). High tech is indeed transforming the way in which we live. It affects labour trends, employment patterns, the development of new products and markets and global and domestic competition.

The central managerial challenge of the future is to design integrated systems that have a reflexive capability built into them. These systems must monitor and match the needs of the high-tech and professional workers with the goals of the firm. This is no easy challenge, since the goal of maximising the productivity of high-tech and professional workers may be at variance with the values of these workers. This managerial challenge must also be played out within the context of unrelenting change.

In assessing key learnings about the management of these workers, it is useful to recap the nature of the high-tech work force, the management of human resources, the management of the culture of the firm, and structural accommodations.

The Nature of the High-Tech Work Force

There are several distinctive features of the high-tech and professional work force. The workers are knowledge workers, and their expertise and talent are in substantial demand by most high-tech firms. These workers have value and attitudinal characteristics that vary significantly from those of other workers. They have invested heavily in their training and specialised knowledge, and they frequently have advanced degrees. They enjoy intellectual and technical challenges—or "puzzles", as Bailyn (1982) refers to them. Since they have expert training and skills, they tend to identify more with their profession or technology than with their employing organisation. This can be a fundamental dilemma for the firm.

In addition, most high-tech and professional workers value and demand autonomy, and most good managers are aware of this. In fact, autonomy serves as a professional reward for many of these workers. They do not consider salary and fringe benefits as important as the meaningfulness of their work. Management must recognise this fact and reward these workers accordingly.

Other values include a strong sense of ethics and an internal performance standard that mitigates against traditional performance appraisal. Professionals identify more with others trained in their technical specialty. Nevertheless, these workers have a strategic importance to the firm that is becoming even more critical with increasing international competition.

High-tech and professional workers cluster in high-tech conglomerations throughout the country, known as technopolii. These technopolii have brought significant changes to the labour markets they serve. Most technopoli have a strong affiliation with a research university, which they depend upon for talent.

Although Belous (1987) and other technological forecasters claim that there is not a general shortage of these high-tech and professional workers, there are indeed shortages in some skill areas that are needed for continued competitiveness. The U.S. government, through its attention to science and technology policy, seems aware of these shortages and committed to providing sufficient engineering and scientific talent to regain technological leadership (Kleingartner and Anderson 1987).

Other distinctive features of high tech are that the production processes are nonroutine, and knowledge is intensive (Gomez-Mejia and Balkin 1985). Many high-tech firms reinvest up to 20 percent of their revenues in R&D because they have a high obsolescence expectancy. Many high-tech firms are young and have been started by an entrepreneurial founder; they remain reasonably flexible in responding to environmental changes. Product life cycles tend to be fairly short and are measured more in terms of months than of years. In fact, most high-tech products have life cycles of approximately one to three years (Gomez-Mejia and Balkin 1985; Miljus and Smith 1987).

In view of the labour requirements for high-tech production, it is fair to say that "the industry tends to go where the costs are lowest...and has tended to expand where there has been a readily available pool of trained scientific and technical workers" (Kleingartner and Anderson 1987:205).

All of these features of the high-tech work force have implications for the way in which a firm's human assets are managed.

The Management of Human Resources

There is an interesting, almost symbiotic, relationship between professional and high-tech workers and high-technology organisations. These firms have a large stake in developing innovative human-resource practices that thoughtfully attract, motivate, and retain these strategically important workers, and that maximise their productivity. Managers must recognise that acertain amount of tension, dissent, and conflict is natural, even when the firm has a well-articulated human-resource philosophy regarding these employees.

A pressing concern for human-resource professionals who must design systems to accommodate high-tech and professional workers is recruiting and training them. Due to the high cost of professional turnover, American industry has begun to put a tremendous amount of funds and energy into training and developmental programs for professionals. More and more, high-tech firms and HR system designers are encouraging professionals to continue their education, either through in-house training and degree-granting programs or through outside universities. HR professionals have recognised the importance of giving these workers "intellectual space", since creativity and innovation are difficult to mandate.

Designing reward systems that encourage the professional's talents is of primary concern. Much attention has been focused on financial incentives as the major means of attracting, motivating, and retaining these workers. Financial rewards have little salience for these workers, however, despite the repeated emphasis in the current literature on pay plans and exquisitely fashioned compensation options.

Instead, professional, career, and content rewards tend to be more valued by these workers. When managers pay attention to the unique characteristics and values of their professional workers, it is less difficult to understand that they are motivated and "driven" to perform by a whole different set of motivators. Critically important here is the challenge and meaningfulness of the work the professional performs. Equally important is that the work retain its meaningfulness over the course of the professional's career. Hence, paying attention to career development is a very important challenge for managers of these workers. Since career development historically has had no more impact than the "pet rock", the design of career-sensitive HR systems is one of the chief design problems of the high-tech firm.

Equally important to professional workers is the design of appropriate performance appraisal systems that are attentive to their standards of evaluation. Since professional workers are largely responsible for new product and process innovations, these employees become the gatekeepers of information. An important challenge for within the context of the firm's culture. As discussed earlier, this requires careful attention to critical design elements that can more appropriately structure the PA event.

Many managers and researchers have downplayed the importance of performance appraisal. Current research, however, indicates that PA need not be demotivational and, in fact, may contribute to goal attainment. When PA fails for professionals, it is typically because of a breakdown in the organisational systems that define, measure, reward, and give feedback on performance. These problems may be identified by critically diagnosing the organisational reward system.

Reward system diagnosis is an extremely important components of this book. The diagnostic activities, questions, and tests presented in chapter represent over a decade of applied research on organisational reward wystems; they should be carefully considered when questions of attraction, motivation, and retention arise. Many of the problems associated with improving the performance of professionals and high-tech workers may be traced to breakdowns in the firm's reward structures and strategies. The culture of the firm plays an imposing role as well.

Management of the Organisation's Culture

The 1980s have seen tremendous emphasis placed on designing and transforming a firm's culture. America has been fascinated with the examination of "culture" and has sought insights from foreign organisational cultures in an effort to isolate the organisational forms that either facilitate or hinder a firm's performance.

When we consider that we are in a crisis of economic productivity, the systematic investigation and dissection of culture has promised economic relief. That promise has not generally been kept, however, the study of culture has shed light on situational ingredients that affect performance. We know that some firms demand a high level of performance from their professional and high-tech workers. That demand can be exciting and challenging for some of the workers in that environment, but it can be debilitating as well. Other high-tech firms resemble "mom-and-pop" companies, with an emphasis more on "family" than on productivity. Each company culture has different HR practices, but none are quite so distinct as the organisational reward systems.

It is the contention here that a given company culture is best supported by integrating HR systems with the culture. This requires determining the fit between different HR practices and the culture of the firm. Most managers seem keen on enhancing creativity and in novations, yet disagree or are unclear on how to achieve this through culture change. To change a firm's culture, or to galvanise workers to achieve excellence, requires systematic consideration of what the desired goals are and an analysis of the HR practices that contribute to or detract from those goals.

Riggs (1983) suggests that the message must be clear as to what the vision of the new culture will be. For example, to stimulate a new product attitude, the message to professionals that new products will be marketed in a steady stream must be clearly stated. In that way, the absence of new products will be understood as the exception to the rule. That attitude must then be reinforced by the design of the reward system. Risk-taking should not be punished, particularly if it results in failure. An engineer managing a group of high-tech and professional employees once said, "If you're not failing, you're not taking risks. If you're not taking risks, then you're not going to be successful in this field."

Attention should be paid to articulating and communicating the vision of the desired culture. Further, systems must be established that reinforce the achievement of goals judged important to the new culture. Those systems involve not only human-resource practices but other structural systems that will enhance productivity.

Structural Accommodations

Since high-tech firms are frequently on the cutting edge of new technologies, it is not surprising that scientists and engineers are now as important as key executives are to traditional firms (Gomez-Mejia and Balkin 1985). These industries are generally characterised by frequent changes, rapid innovations, short product life cycles, and rapid new product developments. They are also known to make quick changes in their work force, their organisational structure, and their operating procedures (Schoonhoven 1986). They are characterised by a very rapid rate and pace of change.

Equally characteristic of high-tech firms are their flexibility, their ability to retain an aura of entrepreneurialism, and their organisation. These firms are fluid and flexible enough to adjust to the enormous number of changes in the external environment.

The messages of the 1960s and 1970s have supported organic structures as the best form for accommodating environmental uncertainty. These messages, however, have been questioned recently; in fact, they have been proven unreliable in view of the swift technological changes that are now quite common to these industries. Unlike traditional firms, which encounter turbulence in their environment in terms of a few products or processes, high-tech firms live in a world of change. As such, the prescription for organic structures is insufficient.

The best-performing firms typically go through a period immediately after start-up when they tend to be flexible and adaptive; however, as they grow, it is critical that they develop clear, reproducible structures, even though a certain amount of structural inertial may thus be institutionalised. This is offset by frequent reorganisations, multiple roles, temporary teams and assignments, and coordination mechanisms based on frequent communications.

High-tech firms also make frequent use of project teams and task forces and have a sparse staff function. Generally, most high-tech firms are constructed along some type of matrix design that allows them to respond quickly to change. They also have small "garage" type or intrapreneurial units that allow flexibility and adaptability as the firm grows in size. The key managerial challenge here is to integrate these various groups within the firm and to be able to change in response to any shift in strategy.

The control systems of high-tech firms resemble collegial control more than standardised control systems. There now is evidence that the more successful high-tech firms follow rational planning processes, even before the actual founding of the firm. Most successful high-tech firms are also fairly decentralised and have reward systems and other H;R systems that are matched with the firm's culture.

When taken as a whole, the structure of the high-tech firm has a chameleon-like quality to it. Successful high-tech firms manage the process of constant change by altering their structures accordingly. They are simultaneously flexible and predictable in their HR practices. They manage the process of new product development and manufacturing with continuity and control, yet they reorganise these processes regularly. They may have a dual ladder to emphasize the importance of the technical experts, or they may even have a triple hierarchy that eases the tension between managers and professionals over resource allocation.

To prepare for the frequent changes, the high-tech firm must have a planning process that is linked directly to its business strategy and, where such exists, to its technology strategy.

Fitness for Future Action

A major challenge facing high-technology firms now and in the future will be developing even greater capacity to meet new challenges. As such, a certain amount of slack is needed in most systems. Further, there needs to be some balance between short-term and longterm priorities. American industry is fond of the bottom-line, which is generally based on short-term performance. We have seen that an overemphasis on the short term can mortgage the future and reduce the likelihood that a firm will be prepared for competition or innovation over the long haul.

Thus, it is imperative that the high-tech firm concentrate its energies on long-term priorities, in addition to demanding short-term results.

In conclusion, managers and the high-tech firms they work for would be well advised to bolster their capacity to meet new challenges in the following ways:

1. *They should recognise that managing high-technology and professional employees is significantly different from managing nonprofessionals.* This is true, in part, because professionals have a different set of values and characteristics, which have been gained through their socialisation in the technical specialty. Managers need to be cognisant of those values and characteristics if they are to anticipate tension points and enhance the fit between the individual and the job.
2. *Managers should recognise that a certain amount of conflict will almost always exist between professionals and hierarchical authority and control systems.* The key is to transform this conflict into motivation by structurally insulating these workers from organisational pressures, while simultaneously making them aware of the importance that their work holds for the firm's well-being and its continued competitive advantage.

3. *They should attempt to develop HR practices and policies that have had some success in attracting, motivating, and retaining the high-tech work force.* That requires, at a minimum, knowledge of or systematic diagnosis of organisational practices, and matching the HR practices to the organisation's culture. It also requires that a cadre of competent HR managers manage the transition. The days of "ready-fire-aim" are over for high-technology firms seeking competitive advantage in their markets.
4. *They should articulate the leader's vision, clearly establish the firm's goals, and ensure that all relevant parties are exposed to that thinking.*
5. *They should design jobs and work relationships to take advantage of technical specialities.* For example, rotating professionals through multiple roles and job responsibilities can sensitise them to new ideas and opportunities.
6. *They should establish career-sensitive tracking systems so that career development becomes an integrated part of their firms practices.*
7. *They should utilise a menu of salient rewards that are relevant for high-tech and professional workers.* These rewards ideally should be linked to performance, but in some cultures they might be linked to effort, risk-taking, or other relevant behaviours.
8. *They should study the change process and learn from their experiences.* High-tech firms change owing to internal and external factors, including departures from tradition, new leaders with new visions, crises or other startling events, key decisions on the part of senior management, or tests of their infrastructural ability to accommodate change. Firms also change because of change. But professionals and other high-tech workers must clearly see the need for change; otherwise, they may not support the change, ro they may even sabotage it. Therefore, communication must be reemphasized.

In conclusion, this book has explored the major issues surrounding the management of high-technology and professional workers. Just as it is difficult to describe a prototypical high-tech or professional worker, so is it difficult to describe the typical high-tech firm. Each firm has a different company culture, and how each firm will respond to the suggestions in this book will undoubtedly vary.

It is fairly clear that there are fundamental diffrences between high-tech firms and more traditional manufacturing firms. High-tech firms tend to be more fluid and therefore more open to expermentation in their human-resource practices (Kleingartner and Anderson 1987). They also tend to be structured differently to accommodate changes. Their success is contingent upon the extent to which they can continuously innovate and design marketable products. This in turn is contingent upon their having the best human talent. We have established that attracting, motivating, and retaining this talent calls for innovative human-resource practices. These practices are best exercised when the firm's reward system is in sync with its culture.

This book should prove most useful to managers and researchers trying to assess the fit between the various components of a high-tech firm and the professionals who work in it. And such, this book should be used as a tool to begin diagnosing, assessing, and researching the effectiveness of the strategies and practices of those firms that are willing and able to meet the challenges in high tech's future.

9

The Commitment in Management

The non-profit organisation exists to bring about a change in individuals and in society. The first thing to talk about is what missions work and what missions don't work, and how to define the mission. For the ultimate test is not the beauty of the mission statement. The ultimate test is right action.

The most common question asked me by non-profit executives is: What are the qualities of a leader? The question seems to assume that leadership is something you can learn in a charm school. But it also assumes that leadership by itself is enough, that it's an end. And that's misleadership. The leader who basically focuses on himself or herself is going to mislead. The three most charismatic leaders in this century inflicted more suffering on the human race than almost any trio in history: Hitler, Stalin, and Mao. What matters is not the leader's charisma. What matters is the leader's mission. Therefore, the first job of the leader is to think through and define the mission of the institution.

Setting Concrete Action Goals

Here is a simple and mundane example—the mission statement of a hospital emergency room: "It's our mission to give assurance to the afflicted." That's simple and clear and direct. Or take the mission of the Girl Scouts of the U.S.A.: to help girls grow into proud, self-confident, and self-respecting young women. There is an Episcopal church on the East Coast which defines its mission as making Jesus the head of this church and its chief executive officer. Or the mission of the Salvation Army, which is to make citizens out of the rejected. Arnold of Rugby, the greatest English educator of the nineteenth century, who created the English public school, defined its mission as making gentlemen out of savages.

My favourite mission definition, however, is not that of a non-profit institution, but of a business. It's a definition that changed Sears from a near-bankrupt, struggling mail-order house at the beginning of the century into the world's leading retailer within less than ten years: It's our mission to be the informed and responsible buyer—first for the American farmer, and later for the American family altogether.

Almost every hospital I know says, "Our mission is health care." And that's the wrong definition. The hospital does not take care of health; the hospital takes care of illness. You and I take care of health by not smoking, not drinking too much, going to bed early, watching our weight, and so on. The hospital comes in when health care breaks down. An even more serious failing of this mission is that nobody can tell you what action or behaviour follows from saying: "Our mission is health care."

A mission statement has to be operational otherwise it's just good intentions. A mission statement has to focus on what the institution really tries to do and then do it so that everybody in the organisation can say, This is *my* contribution to the goal.

Many years ago, I sat down with the administrators of a major hospital to think through the mission statement of the emergency room. It took us a long time to come up with the very simple, and (most people thought) too obvious statement that the emergency room was there to give assurance to the afflicted. To do that well, you have to know what really goes on. And, much to the surprise of the physicians and nurses, it turned out that in a good emergency room, the function is to tell eight out of ten people there is nothing wrong that a good night's sleep won't take care of. You've been shaken up. Or the baby has the flu. All right, it's got convulsions, but there is nothing seriously wrong with the child. The doctors and nurses give assurance.

We worked it out, but it sounded awfully obvious. Yet translating that mission statement into action meant that everybody who comes in is now seen by a qualified person in less than a minute. That is the mission; that is the goal. The rest is implementation. Some people are immediately rushed to intensive care, others get a lot of tests, and yet others are told: "Go back home, go to sleep, take an aspirin, and don't worry. If these things persist, see a physician tomorrow." But the first objective is to see everybody, almost immediately—because that is the only way to give assurance.

The task of the non-profit manager is to try to convert the organisation's mission statement into specifics. The mission may be forever—or at least as long as we can foresee. As long as the human race is around, we'll be be miserable sinners. As long as the human race is around, there will be sick people. And, as long as the human race is around, there will be alcoholics and drug addicts and the unfortunate. For hundreds of years we've had schools of one kind or another trying to get a little knowledge into seven year old boys and girls who would rather be out playing.

But the goal can be short-lived; or it might change drastically because a mission is accomplished. A hundred years ago, one of the great inventions of the late nineteenth century was the tuberculosis sanatorium. That mission has been accomplished, at least in developed countries. We know how to treat TB with antibiotics. And so managers of non-profits also have to build in review, revision, and organised abandonment. The mission is forever and may be divinely ordained; the goals are temporary.

One of our most common mistakes is to make the mission sttement into a kind of hero sandwich of good intentions. It has to be simple and clear. As you add new tasks, you deemphasize and get rid of old ones. You can only do so many things. Look at what we are trying to do in our colleges. The mission statement is confused—we are trying to do fifty different things. It won't work, and that's why the fundamentalist colleges attract so many young people. Their mission is very narrow. You and I may quarrel with it and say it's too narrow, but it's clear. It enables the students to understand. And it also enables the faculty to know. And it enables that administration to say, We aren't going to teach accounting.

As you add on, you have to abandon. But you also have to think through which are the few things we can accomplish that will do the most for us, and which are the things that contribute either marginally or are no longer of great significance. A hundred years ago, about the greatest contribution the hospital could make was in obstetrics, though it took a long time before the population accepted that, because childbirth at home in the growing city was perceived to be, well, dangerous, what with infection and untrained people. Well, now I would say that not every hospital should do obstetrics, and a great many don't. Partly because it's become so much safer, so much more predictable. But also because if anything does go wrong, it's so much more critical, so you need a concentration of resources. In a suburban community there just might not be enough volume to do a really good job. So perhaps you don't abandon obstetrics, but you phase it out slowly. On the other hand, fifty or sixty years ago, before the psychotropic drugs, no hospital could do much for mental diseases. Today, almost a majority of people who are mentally sick or endangered can be taken care of in the community hospital, with short-term stays for depression and so on. You can make a major contribution there.

So you constantly look at the state-of-the-art. You look at the opportunities in the community. The hospital isn't going to sell shoes and it's not going into education on a big scale. It's going to take care of the sick. But the specific objective may change. Things that were of primary importance may become secondary or even totally irrelevant. You must watch this constantly, or else very soon you will become a museum piece.

The Three "Musts" of a Successful Mission

Look at strength and performance. Do better what you already do well—if it's the right thing to do. The belief that every institution can do everything is just not true. When you violate the values of an institution, you are likely to do a poor job. In the 1960s, all of us in academia rushed into the urban problem. We were totally incompetent: our values don't fit what are political issues; academicians don't understand power. At the same time, hospitals rushed into what they called health education. Here are the people who come in, such as the diabetic, and before they go home maybe we can teach them how to handle their diet and their stress and so on so that they don't come back. It hasn't worked. That's not what hospitals are good at. Hospitals are *not* good at prevention; hospitals are good at taking care of damage that's already been done.

Look outside at the opportunities, the needs. Where can we, with the limited resources we have—and I don't just mean people and money, but also competence—really make a difference, really set a new standard? One sets the standard by doing something and doing it well. You create a new dimension of performance.

The next thing to look at is what we really believe in. A mission is not, in that sense, impersonal. I have never seen anything being done well unless people were committed.

All of us know the story of the Edsel automobile. Everybody thinks the Edsel failed because Ford didn't do its homework. In fact, it was the best-engineered, the best-researched, the best-everything car. There was only one thing wrong with it: nobody in the Ford Motor Company believed in it. It was contrived. It was designed on the basis of research and not on the basis of commitment. And so when it got into a little trouble, nobody supported the child. I'm not saying it could have been a success. But without that personal commitment, it certainly never could be a success.

And so one asks first, what are the opportunities, the needs? Then, do they fit us? Are we likely to do a decent job? Are we competent? Do they match our strengths? Do we really believe in this? This is not just true of products, it's true of services.

So, you need three things: opportunities; competence; and commitment. Every mission statement, believe me, has to reflect all three or it will fall down on what is its ultimate goal, its ultimate purpose and final test. It will not mobilise the human resources of the organisation for getting the right things done.

10

The Practice of Decision Making

Executives, whether in a non-profit institution or in a business, actually spend little time on decision making. Far more of their time is spent in meetings, with people, or in trying to get a little information. Yet it's in the decision that everything comes together. That is the make or break point of the organisation. Most of the other tasks executives do, other people could do. But only executives can make the decisions. And they either make decisions effectively or they render themselves ineffective.

The least effective decision makers are the ones who constantly make decisions. The effective ones make very few. They concentrate on the important decisions. And even people who work hard on making decisions often misapply their time. They slight the important decisions and spend excessive time making easy—or irrelevant—decisions.

The most important part of the effective decision is to ask: what is the decision really about? Very rarely is a decision about what it seems to be about. That's usually a symptom.

Some twenty years ago, a Girl Scout Council in a major suburban area realised that the ethnic composition of the area was changing rapidly. It had been lily-white, and so had the Scouts. But now the area was rapidly becoming highly diverse: blacks, Hispanics, Asians were arriving in large numbers. That the Council had to offer scouting to the children of the newcomers was obvious to everyone. But so was the enormous cost of providing scouting to very poor neighbourhoods. The question that seemed to demand a decision was, therefore, seen as a financial one: How do we raise the money? And the answer to that question seemed obvious: Have separate troops for different ethnic groups. Otherwise, it was feared, financial support from the affluent group, the whites, might be endangered.

Fortunately, one of the leaders then asked: What is this decision all about? Is our mission to raise money, or is it to build a nation? It was clear at once that the decision was one of basic principle, to be decided contrary to all of the Council's precedents. The answer had to be that, whatever the financial risk, we are not going to have ethnic troops. That is the past. We have to emphasize that young women are young women—not black, not white, not Italian not Jewish, not Vietnamese—but young American women. That is what the decision was really all about. Once this was clear, the decision made itself. And the whole community accepted that decision without a murmur, once it was explained.

A major university with severe budget problems had to accept that it must cut programs. But which ones? At first, this was seen as a financial decision: where do we spend the most? The ensuing civil war within the faculty almost destroyed the institution. But then one board member said, "We are tackling the wrong issue. We should be discussing whether to put our major emphasis on the continuing education of adults or whether to stick with teaching the young. That's what this decision is about. The rest is implementation." Suddenly it became clear why people had been so hot under the collar. The decision was not about the budget but about the future of American higher education and the university's role in it, and this is something on which good people *should* disagree. Such a decision is a strategic decision, and halfway measures won't do. If the university's future is in continuing education, it is not going to cut. It has to go out and raise the money; otherwise, it has no future.

Decisions always involve risk taking. And effective decisions take a lot of time and thought. For this reason, one doesn't make unnecessary decisions. Again and again, non-profit institutions go through a painful reorganisation, moving staff and activities around because two people are feuding with one another. But they have been feuding for twenty years and will keep on feuding what ever the organisation structure. Leave them alone.

And don't make decisions on trivia. I live sixty miles east of Los Angeles, with four freeways into the city. They all have the same mileage; it's totally unpredictable which one will be jammed. Whether you take one or the other is not a decision. Routine decisions are decisions that have no consequences, or at least no foreseeable consequences. Don't waste time on them.

Opportunity and Risk

The next question in decision making is opportunity versus risk. One starts out with the opportunity, not with the risk: If this works, what will it do for us? Then look at the risks. And there are three kinds of risks:

There is the risk we can afford to take. If it goes wrong, it is easily reversible with minor damage. Then there is the irreversible decision, when failure may do serious harm. Finally there is the decision where the risk is great but one cannot afford *not* to take it. Here's an example. Forty years ago a Brooklyn neighbourhood in New York radically changed from white working class to a black slum. A major hospital in the area almost overnight became empty, going down to about 12 percent occupancy. Its regular physicians had left with their patients. Keeping the hospital open could not be economically justified but the community needed its services. The decision—and it was bitterly fought—was to keep the hospital open and to raise the money somehow for the three to five years until the hospital's patient base could be rebuilt. The decision came very close to total disaster. But to stay open was a risk the hospital had to take if it wanted to maintain its mission.

The Need for Dissent

All the first-rate decision makers I've observed, beginning with Franklin D. Roosevelt, had a very simple rule: If you have consensus on an important matter, don't make the decision. Adjourn it so that everybody has a little time to think. Important decisions are risky. They *should* be controversial. Acclamation means that nobody has done the homework.

Because it is essential in an effective discussion to understand what it is really about, there has to be dissent and disagreement. If you make a decision by acclamation, it is almost bound to be made on the apparent symptoms rather than on the real issue. You need dissent; but you have to make it productive.

About seventy years ago, an American political scientist, Mary Parker Follet, said that when you have dissent in an organisation, you should never ask *who* is right. You should not even ask *what* is right. You must assume that each faction gives the right answer, but to a different question. Each sees a different reality.

A few years ago, as we saw earlier, a major hospital was torn by internal conflict within its medical staff. One group advocated moving the eye clinic out of the hospital. Most eye operations have become ambulatory and it is far more economical to do them where they do not have to carry the whole overhead of the big hospital. The other group saw such a move as the first step toward complete restructuring of the hospital. Both were right, but both saw only part of the reality.

Instead of arguing what is right, assume that each faction has the right answer. But which question is each trying to answer? Then, you gain understanding. You also gain, in many cases, the ability to bring the two together in a synthesis. Then you can say: In this case we are not deciding on ophthalmology; that is just an incident. But the decision to move the eye clinic out commits us to restructuring the hospital. If we believe that moving out of the hospital is tomorrow's right structure, let's not talk economics, whether of the hospital or of eye surgery. And everybody understands it. Look upon dissent as a means of creating understanding and mutual respect.

Emotions always run high over any decision in which the organisation is at risk if that decision fails, or in one that is not easily reversible. The smart thing is to treat this as constructive dissent and as a key to mutual understanding.

If you can bring dissent and disagreement to a common understanding of what the discussion is all about, you create unity and commitment. There is a very old saying—it goes back all the way to Aristotle and later on became an axiom of the early Christian Church: In essentials unity, in action freedom, and in all things trust. And trust requires that dissent come out into the open, and that it be seen as honest disagreement.

This is particularly important for non-profit institutions, which have a greater propensity for internal conflict than businesses precisely because everybody is committed to a good cause. Disagreement isn't just a matter of your opinion versus mine, it is your good faith versus mine. Non-profit institutions, therefore, have to be particularly careful not to become riddled by feuds and distrust. Disagreements must be brought out into the open and taken seriously.

A second reason to encourage dissent is that any organisation needs a nonconformist. If and when things change, it needs somebody who is willing and able to change. This is not the kind of person who says, "There is a right way and a wrong way—and our way." Rather, he or she asks, "What is the right way *now?*" You don't want only yes-men or yes-women. You want a critic—and one the organisation respects.

Bringing disagreement into the open also enables non-profit executives to brush aside the unnecessary, the meaningless, the trivial conflict. It enables them to concentrate on the real issues. When you bring conflicts out in the open, a good many disappear. People realise that they are trivia and not that serious. Yes, there is a conflict. You here in the surgery see one thing and you here in internal medicine see another. But is this pertinent to *this* specific case? If not, you say what our teacher of religion said to us when we were thirteen: "Boys, kill each other, but not in my class." Fight it out outside; it doesn't belong here. You don't resolve the conflict, but you do make it irrelevant. If you can do that, you are way ahead.

Another example: I was present, not so long ago, at a meeting at a museum that degenerated into civil war. People were screaming at each other until one of the wise old men pointed out that the two groups were both right. One, in arguing for a big new building, assumed the kind of museum we are now building, which is a museum that is a community asset. So, members of this group assumed we were talking about a tremendous expansion. The other group assumed the opposite. It wanted to concentrate on a very small number of real masterpieces and create a standard of excellence in which every single object was the best in its class, which is very much the way the great nineteenth-century collectors went about their business. The word "museum" was the same, but that was the only thing.

Once the position of each group was understood, it became clear that the conflict had nothing to do with the matter under discussion. Sooner or later a decision will be made to go one way or the other, and then half the board will resign—may be to start a new museum. But that wasn't what we had to decide at that meeting. Suddenly there was peace, harmony, even laughter.

Conflict Resolution

You use dissent and disagreement to resolve conflict. If you ask for disagreement openly, it gives peopel the feeling that they have been heard. But you also know where the objectors are and what their objections are. And in many cases you can accommodate them, so that they can accept the decision gracefully. That also enables them very often to understand the arguments of the winning side. Maybe not to *accept* them: but to see that these people are neither stupid nor malicious. They only differ. In this way you resolve conflict. You do not prevent disagreement, but you do resolve conflict.

Another way to resolve conflict is to ask the two people who most vocally oppose each other, especially if both of them are respected community members, to sit down and work out a common approach. They do this by starting out with the areas in which they agree.

The third way is by defusing the argument. You say, "Let's start out by finding out what we *agree* on." Then disagreements often turn out to be peripheral. On essentials there is common ground and you can work out things. In some cases you say, "Let's split the difference", or, "Let's postpone this", or, "Is this really that important?" You play down the areas of disagreement and play up the areas of agreement.

These are by no means new techniques; there are examples in the Old Testament. Finding common ground especially is what the elders of any tribe do to maintain unity. One cannot prevent conflict. But one can make it—I wouldn't say irrelevant, but secondary. And the best tool for this is the constructive use of dissent.

From Decision to Action

A decision is a commitment to action. But far too many decisions remain pious intentions. There are four common causes for this. One is that we try to "sell" the decision rather than to "market" it. In the West, we tend to make the decision fast—and then we start to "sell" it to the people in the organisation. That takes three years, and by the time the decision has been "bought", it has become obsolete. Here we can learn from the Japanese. They build the implementation in *before* they make the decision. In the Japanese organisation, everyone who will be affected by the decision—and especially everyone who will have to do something to carry it out—is asked to comment on the issue before that decision is made. This looks incredibly slow. Westerners watching the process climb up the walls. But then the Japanese make the decision—the point at which we in the West begin to "Sell." Not so the Japanese, Bingo! The next day everyone understands it, everyone acts on it.

A second way to lose the decision is to go systemwide immediately with the new policy or the new service. This jumps the testing stage. We disregard what Frances Hesselbein of the Girl Scouts told us in her interview in this book: Find the targets of opportunity in your non-profit institution and concentrate on them. Don't try to convert everybody right away.

I like to try the new in three different places with three different people—something I learned forty years ago from the people who introduced physical therapy in the American hospital. There was almost u niversal resistance to the idea. Most hospitals said it was none of their business. The innovators didn't even try to convert the non-believers. They picked three hospitals in three communities that were eager to do physical therapy: a large teaching hospital with many older people, stroke victims, and so on; a small semi-rural hospital that had lots of industrial and farming accidents; and a fair-sized suburban comunity hospital with a lot of ordinary cases, broken bones, arthritis, and so on. They worked only with these three hospitals for five years. By then, every hospital in the country wanted physical therapy.

But by then, also, the product had become quite different from the original design. The three pilots showed, for instance, that psychological counseling and work with the patient's family are just as important in rehabilitation as exercise and physiology—something which had not even occurred to the innovators but which made an enormous difference in effectiveness. In industry we learned long ago that we are going to be in trouble if we jump the pilot stage. We have to learn that this is just as true for social projects and services.

The third caveat: no decision has been made until someone is designated to carry it out. Someone has to be accountable—

with a work plan, a goal, and a deadline. Decisions don't make themselves effective; people do.

Finally—common mistake number four—I've seen wonderful decisions come a cropper because nobody really thought through who had to do what. In what form should the decision be communicated to each person who has to implement that decision so that he or she can actually act? What training does each need? What tools? I have seen a decision couched in a brilliant mathematical model which forklift drivers in the warehouse were expected to carry out. It didn't become effective. You not only have to translate a decision into the language of the people who have to do the work; you also have to fit it into their assumptions. You have to build the new behaviour into their instructions, their training, their compensation. And then you have to follow up. Don't depend on reports. Go to the warehouse and look. Otherwise, you'll find a year later that nothing has happened.

Every decision is a commitment of present resources to the uncertainties of the future. This, according to elementary probability mathematics, means that decisions will turn out to be wrong more often than right. At the least they will have to be adjusted. Practically every single decision American hospitals made in the sixties and seventies has been shot out of the water by changes in government—particularly reimbursement policies on Medicare. As a result, hospitals suddenly have a surplus of beds. But that's a normal outcome for decisions on the future.

The decision always has to be bailed out. That requires two things. First, that you think through alternatives ahead of time so that you have something to fall back on if and when things go wrong. Second, that you build into the decision the responsibility for bailing it out, instead of going in and arguing about who made what mistakes. One weakness of non-profit institutions is that they believe that they have to be infallible—far more so than businesses. Businesses somehow know mistakes are being made. In non-profit institutions, mistakes are not permitted. And so if something goes wrong, a court-martial begins. Whose fault is it? Instead, we need to ask, Who is going to bail this out? Who is going to redirect the program or operation, and how?

11

Reward Systems and Company Culture

Consistent runners-up find their obs gone.
–A pepsico manager
You have to shoot the president to get fired.
–A UPI manager

These two quotations from a *Business Week* article suggest two very different types of corporate cultures and reward systems. The culture of PepsiCo has historically placed great value on competitive success, rewarding winners and ousting losers. Employees in that setting have a reasonably clear set of guidelines about what they must do to merely survive, and what they must do to prosper. The corporate culture of UPI is one of paternalism, and one in which almost anything would be tolerated. Both draw our attention to an important fact of organisational life—that a company's culture and reward system are not only interdependent but they feed off each other. With minor exceptions, this fact has rarely been acknowledged in the management literature (Sethia and Von Glinow 1984; Kerr and Slocum 1987).

The purpose of this chapter is to focus attention on the culture-reward system relationship and to highlight the implications of this relationship for managing high-tech and professional employees.

The Twin Concepts

Corporate Culture

Most of us have a somewhat intuitive feel for corporate culture; the subject has captured the attention of practitioners and scholars alike in the 1980s. While there are no absolute definitions of organisational culture, the following offer common themes.

Peters and Waterman (1982) talk about culture as the shared values of the company's members. Kilmann (1982) calls it the "collective will of members...indicating what the corporation really wants or what really counts in order to get ahead." Schein (1983) refers to it as the "sum total of the collective or shared learnings of a group.". For purposes of discussion, I am using the Sethia and Von Glinow (1985) definition: "Culture is the shared and relatively enduring pattern of basic values, beliefs, and assumptions in an organisation" (p. 403).

As described chapter, "organisational reward system" refers to interrelated elements: the types of rewards that are available, the conditions under which these rewards are made available to members, and the ways in which the rewards and the criteria are administered. If an organisation's culture involves the basic values, assumptions, and beliefs of its members, the twin concept is that culture is influential in determining the types of rewards that are available in an organisation, the conditions under which the rewards are allocated to groups or individuals, the way in which the rewards and their criteria are selected, and the manner in which the total reward system is administered (Sethia and Von Glinow 1985; Von Glinow 1985).

Often the impact of a firm's culture is quite direct; such an impact can be seen in ruthlessly performance-oriented cultures, such as PepsiCo, where rewards are based solely on certain aspects of performance. A firm's culture can influence its reward system indirectly through its human-resource philosophy and practices. Much of the substance of culture is "concerned with controlling the behaviours and attitudes of organisation members, and the reward system is a primary method of achieving control" (Kerr and Slocum 1987: 99). HR philosophies and practices that are sensitive to the high-technology and professional employee underly corporate policies such as "job content rewards, peer appraisals, career development, duel ladders and autonomous working environments" (Von Glinow 1985: 194). Firms like IBM, AT&T, and Hewlett-Packard have well-developed HR philosophies—articulated through their credos—that impact the reward practices of these firms. Hewlett-Packard's practices

Figure 11.1. The Culture-Reward System Relationship.

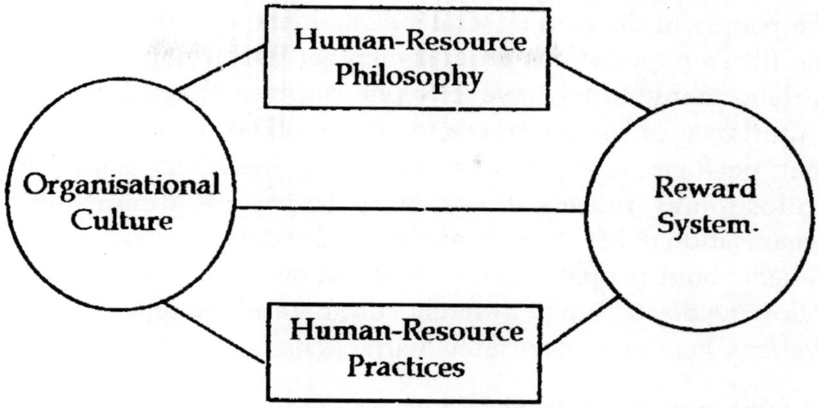

include no layoffs, long-term incentives and rewards, and incentives that are companywide. Figure 11.1 illustrates the relationships between culture and reward systems.

The twin concepts are highly intertwined. Stonich (1984) notes that current culture is a function of past reward policies. Lawler (1983) notes that the reward system can reinforce and help define the organisational structure. That is, the reward system can help define the degree to which technical professionals can influence line management, and it can strongly influence the kind of decisionmaking structure that exists. In short, reward systems can shape culture because they influence motivation, satisfaction, and membership. "The behaviours they cause to occur become the dominant patterns of behaviour in the organisation and lead to perceptions and beliefs about what an organisation stands for, believes in, and values" (Lawler 1983:11).

Until recently, Chase Manhattan Bank was not particularly performance-driven and "rewarded people more for appearance than performance", which resulted in "inbreeding and a smugness that made the bank loathe to grapple with competitors" (*Business Week* 1980: 158). Thus, a company's culture and its reward system must be in a balanced relationship for the company to function smoothly (Sethia and Von Glinow 1985).

But particular types of organisational cultures appear to function best with particular types of reward systems. The matching combinations fall into four very distinguishable patterns

(Sethia and Von Glinow 1985; Von Glinow 1985). These patterns are based on two important positions: the firm's concern about the people in the firm as vital stakeholders; and the intensity of the firm's expectations around member performance. As noted earlier, many firms have HR philosophies that focus on the importance of human assets, whereas others focus on the role that performance plays. Though not interchangeable, both philosophies represent two very important dimensions of organisational life, which are fundamental to our discussion. Beliefs about people and beliefs about performance underly the following discussion of different cultures and the types of reward systems generally associated with each.

A Typology of Different Cultures

As discussed, the underpinnings of a company's culture are revealed by its human-resource orientation. Therefore, company cultures may be differentiated and classified by examining their concern for human assets and their concern for performance. Concern for human assets refers to the firm's commitment to the well-being of its members and its respect for their values, attitudes, and beliefs. Concern for performance refers to the firm's expectation that its members will give their personal best on their jobs.

We can discern the following typology of organisational cultures: a low or high level of concern for human assets, coupled with a low or high level of concern for performance, suggests four generic types of organisational cultures, which are grounded in the HR orientations of each type (Sethia and Von Glinow 1985). These four types, as shown in Figure 11.2, are the apathetic culture, the caring culture, the exacting culture, and the integrative culture.

The apathetic culture shows relatively little concern for the firm's human assets and indifference to their performance. The caring culture shows high concern for people as assets and has relatively undemanding performance expectations. The exacting culture exhibits little sensitivity to the people of the firm, but has demanding and exacting performance expectations. The integrative culture shows high concern for people and has high performance expectations.

Figure 11.2. Framework of Human-Resource Cultures.

Concern for People		Low	High
	High	Caring	Integrative
	Low	Apathetic	Exacting
		Concern for Performance	

In general and somewhat contrary to the thinking of Sethia and Von Glinow (1985)—these cultures support a variety of reward systems. Each culture, however, is optimally compatible with only one specific type of reward system. The reward systems that seem to be compatible with each of the four cultures are summarised in Table 11.1.

The Apathetic Culture

Apathetic cultures are inherently counter-rational. Such firms lack concern for people and are indifferent to their performance. Apathetic firms seem to operate in moral vacuums, with inept or alienated leadership. Clearly, the long-term prospects for such firms are problematic; but they may survive if they have a monopolistic position in their industry or are protected by law.

An example of the apathetic culture is the one that prevailed at RCA until recently. According to *Business Week* (1984), in a cover article the company historically was "dominated by Byzantine cabals, factions, and schisms", and during that time, "talk of who was up and who was down occupied the troops far more than the company's business." Apparently, there were reports of "bureaucratic hacks who had built power bases by virtue of long tenure" (p. 53). Top aides were hired and publicly fired, but they were "compensated handsomely both coming in and going out" (p. 54). Some analysts suggested that the denigration of people and the neglect of performance for so many years literally drained the vitality of this pioneer in radio and television.

Table 11.1.

Compatibility of Reward Systems with Four Culture.

	Human-Resource Cultures			
Reward Systems	*Apathetic*	*Caring*	*Exacting*	*Integrative*
1. *Types of Reward*				
Financial	Low	Average	Variable	Excellent
Status	Excellent	Excellent	Moderate	Low
Job Content	Poor	Average	Good	Excellent
Career	Poor	Good	Average	Excellent
Professional	Poor	Average	Good	Excellent
2. *Sample Criteria for Reward*				
Performance: results	Individual success illusory	Reasonable effort day-to-day	Individual success short-term	Individual/group firm success long-term
Performance: actions and behaviours	Manipulation; politicking	Compliance; cooperation	Efficiency; competition	Innovation; independence
Nonperformance considerations	Contract; patronage	Member; position	Nature of work; costs of replacement	Equity; potential

Source: Adapted from Nirmal Sethia and Mary Ann Von Glinow, "Arriving at Four Cultures by Managing the Reward System", in Kilmann, Saxton, Serpa and Associates, ed., *Gaining Control of the Corporate Culture* (San Francisco: Jossey-Bass, 1985).

While there are other reported examples of apathetic cultures, they are not as common among high-tech businesses operating in highly competitive environments with narrow profit margins. Instead, this culture is more apt to be found in strong monopolies, cartels, some public-sector organisations, and state-owned enterprises in some countries. In these types of organisations, entrenched interests prevail, as do political expediencies and ideological proclivities.

An examination of the reward strategies used to attract, motivate, and retain high-tech and professional workers reveals that apathetic firms offer a considerable amount of job security. In some cases, lucrative contracts are offered. To attract qualified professionals, these types of companies rarely use the term "performance-oriented", but instead rely on matters of custom ("We've always done it that way") or on patronage (Von Glinow 1985). Since the company perceives that it has no real competition, the recruiting pitch may not focus on productivity. Knowing that a firm is not terribly bottomline-driven can appeal to some high-tech and professional workers. This environment may appeal to those who are not risk-oriented, or to those who do not really care to work on product innovations that must meet some competitive standard ro be held up to strict scrutiny.

In this type of culture, financial rewards are generally poor to average, although in some cases, as mentioned above, the financial rewards may be more generous. Job content rewards seem relatively difficult to come by in this type of company. Career rewards—principally job security—are high, but promotions are generally slow. Growth opportunities appear rather limited. Status rewards are usually limited to a privileged few and are highly visible.

To retain professionals in this culture, strategies revolve around showing professionals how they may capitalise upon the absence of certain factors (for example, lack of performance standards or competitive threats). This culture may appeal to those professionals and high-tech workers who are more politically oriented or power-driven than others, since the ability to play politics and hide behind the "rules" is its own reward (Von Glinow 1985). Professional rewards, however, like job content rewards, are generally missing; the commitment that professionals have to their specialty is not particularly valued in the apathetic culture.

Since, by definition, performance is not deemed important, most rewards are likely to come from meeting one's contractual obligations, or from patronage. Some individuals may use what they perceive as their personal accomplishments to bargain for rewards although such accomplishments are generally more illusory than real. Actions and behaviours that pay off include politicking, manipulating rules, and the like.

The Caring Culture

Like the apathetic culture, the caring culture has weak performance expectations of its professionals. This culture, however, is very concerned about its employees; its attitude can border on the paternalistic. The traditional cultures of firms like AT&T, Bank of America, and Corning Glass are representative of this type of culture. As long as the environment poses no real competitive threat, these firms can function quite smoothly, since employees readily comply with organisational leaders. The people may be said to be extremely loyal.

The types of rewards that are available to attract, motivate, and retain professionals generally play up the "human side of the company [as exhibited] through its management practices" (Von Glinow 1985:198). These companies highlight job security, career rewards, and the sense of working for a firm that is trustworthy and fair. In general, training and development programs within these cultures are good. Status rewards tend to be substantial, but as with the apathetic culture, job content and professional rewards tend to be on the low end. Financial rewards tend to be average, by market standard. To attract professionals, the caring culture company offers incentives such as geographical location, a good school district, and child-care facilities. In addition, some front-end bonuses are given.

Given the trend toward dual-career families, it should be noted that most of the rewards offered by caring cultures tend to focus on individual professional needs. If these companies have attracted professionals who do not want intrusions into their autonomy, they need to offer some degree of autonomy to motivate such professionals to stay.

Retention is a key cocnern, and these firms frequently engage their professional staff in attitude and morale surveys. Also, opportunities for training and development are common, as are programs designed to upgrade skills and education. Caring companies also try to retain professionals by promoting from within and by using perquisities for those in senior ranks. In addition, we would expect these companies to have strong pension programs and programs that allow professionals to phase-retire if they choose.

Since conditions for rewards are not particularly performance based—although people are expected to make reasonable efforts in their daily work—some actions and behaviours are more likely than others to influence the employee's rewards. For example, teamwork, cooperation, conformity, and "playing it safe" would be rewarded. Similarly, politicking, manipulation, and taking risks would not be rewarded.

Many rewards in the caring culture are membership-based, while other rewards are governed mainly by tenure and position in the firm's hierarchy. The personnel policies of Bank of America have been labeled "traditional" and have been likened to those of the civil service; one corporate officer observed that "everybody at a certain grade could could expect about the same salary and the same increase" (Zonana 1984: 1).

The Exacting Culture

This is the culture that might be described as "performance-driven", or success-oriented. In this cultural pattern, performance is what counts and individuals are sometimes expendable (Sethia and Von Glinow 1985). Employees are expected to perform at a sustained level of high performance, epitomised by Grove's (1983) description of Intel, where people are expected to do their "personal best."

Some likely possibilities here include PeopsiCo, Texas Instruments, ITT during the reign of Geneen, Intel, and Emerson Electric, where nothing is said to be more sacred than the bottom line (*Business Week* 1983).

In these cultures, financial rewards are generally substantial. These include profit-sharing, front-end bonuses, and stock options, coupled with special award and recognition bonuses associated with successful performance. The exacting culture makes a point of "being Number One", of "going or the best." Emerson Electric, for example, rewards superachievers handsomely. "Divisional managers can increase their annual compensation up to 81 percent by exceeding present goals" (*Business Week* 1983:61).

Job content and professional rewards can be high in the exacting culture because the professional must utilise exceptional expertise and skill in meeting and exceeding performance expectations. While status rewards vary from company to company, there is prestige associated with being with the best firm. Job security tends to be low, and other career rewards are moderate, since a professional's security is strictly dependent upon how well he or she performs. This results-oriented emphasis precludes meaningful employee development programs, thus contributing to rapid burnout (Sethia and Von Glinow 1985).

The availability of rewards in the exacting culture is highly contingent upon the results of the professional's efforts. Also, the shorterm emphasis generally outweighs any long-term focus. The types of actions and behaviours that pay off tend to be predicated on success. Almost anything goes, as long as it is successful. Hoarding of resources, withholding information, and not taking risks may be rewarded—as long as these actions and behaviours produce successful results. Taking risks and being innovative and creative are ostensibly rewarded in this culture; however, they can be discouraged by the penalties associated with failure. Nonperformance criteria generally do not determine the rewards in the exacting culture.

The Integrative Culture

This culture category matches high concern for people with strong performance expectations. The net result is a blend of values; professionals are considered capable of significant contributions to the overall goals of the firm, as well as to their own goals. The integrative culture appears to offer above-average rewards of all types—with the exception of status rewards—to attract, motivate, and retain high-technology and professional employees. The integrative culture values people and attempts to challenge them in meaningful ways.

IBM, Hewlett-Packard, and Tandem Computers fit this culture category. Employees are considered capable of making significant contributions to these firms and are expected to do so. The performance expectation is not paternalistic or demanding, but concentrates on the dignity of people. At Hewlett-Packard; for example, they "recruit the best talent from the best engineering schools...[and] move young engineers quickly into significant jobs in an informal environment" (*Business Week* 1982:78).

Available rewards include offering professionals well—above-average compensation and benefits to initially attract and subsequently retain them. In addition, profit-sharing, stock options, and bonuses are commonly used. Unlike any of the other cultures, professional rewards that link the professional's abilities and expertise to the mission of the firm are well-known.

Integrative firms think about the subsequent training, development, or education that the professional will need. These companies typically promise appropriate career movement (whether in a managerial or a technical specialty) that is predicated on meeting or exceeding company goals. Enlarged jobs and considerable job responsibility are offered to attract professionals who are known to thrive on challenges that are neither too hard nor too easy to achieve (Von Glinow 1985).

Performance is a core value in the integrative culture; thus, significant rewards are contingent upon performance. Performance may be expected of the individual, the group, or the firm, depending on the nature of the jobs. Performance is not viewed, however, solely "in terms of the current bottom line, but long-term implications are also taken into consideration. Actions and behaviours that are valued in the Integrative culture include self-management, cooperation, risk taking, innovation, experimentation and skill building" (Sethia and Von Glinow 1985:415). Nonperformance rewards may be given for equity purposes or for individual potential.

Strategic Implications for Reward System Design

Table 11.2 presents the combinations of reward strategies that typify each of the four categories of culture.

Not all high-tech firms employing professionals will fit neatly into one of the four categories. Further, a firm may encompass subcultures that resemble one of the four categories while the overall firm resembles a different category. Thus, multiple reward systems can coexist in a given culture category. The purpose of culture categorisation is to isolate some of the strategic implications involved in the design of reward systems. The culture categories permit a somewhat deeper analysis and understanding of the organisational realities associated with the employment of professionals.

Table 11.2.

Reward Strategies for Organisational Cultures

Culture	*Attraction/Motivation*	*Retention*
Apathetic	No bottom-line emphasis Job security Contracts Matters of custom; patronage Personality; risk-averse	Concentrate on job security and autonomy Appeal to the politically oriented professionals
Caring	People-oriented; job security Trustworthiness and fairness Flexible benefits	Training and development programs Continuing education programs Liberalisation of retirement benefits Seniority or tenure-based rewards
Exacting	Financial rewards Bonuses Job content rewards Performance-and success-driven	Profit-sharing Stock ownership Emphasis on entrepreneurial spirit Garage-type inde- pendent business units
Integra--tive	Above-average compensation and benefits Job security Job content rewards Quick advancement opportunities	Skill-based pay Advancement opportunities readily available Tailor-made Challenging Task-relevant feedback

Source: Adapted from Mary Ann Von Glinow, "Reward Strategies for Attracting, Evaluating, and Retaining Professionals", *Human Resource Management* 24, no. 2 (Summer 1985). © 1985 by John Wiley & Sons, Inc.

Therefore, the following implications can be drawn:

1. *Culture change requires a change in the reward system.* Given that multiple reward systems may coexist in any given culture, it is useful to determine a priori which rewards the culture best supports. Since most high-tech firms engage in culture change to meet competitive threats, it is vital to assess what kinds of rewards and what levels of rewards will best support the desired culture. Reward system change is an integral part of culture change. Given the different forces behind culture change—including changes in company strategy, technology, work values, leadership, and regulatory policy, all discussed earlier—a parallel change in the company's reward system enhances the likelihood that the culture change will be successful.
2. *Changes involving the reward system must account for the unique role of the professional and high-technology employee.* The salience of rewards has long been a factor in attracting, motivating, and retaining professional employees. Different reward wystems should be seriously considered (Von Glinow 1985), particularly in any reward system change effort.
3. *Reward system design should be tailored to specific cultures and organisational situations.* The tailoring of any system does not occur in a vacuum, but rather, resembles aiming at a moving target. As such, it may discourage systematic diagnosis and design. But there are numerous cases where some very innovative reward systems failed to impact organisational performance simply because they did not fit the culture of the firm. System designers should take a critical look at the existing culture to determine if and how the culture is desirable. Given the peculiarities of the different cultures, care should be taken to match the professional with the cultural setting and the reward system. Changes in strategic reward system design argue for morre fluid change approaches, as discussed in detail later.

12

Teaching Management

Knowing-in-Action

I use the term *professional artistry* to refer to the kinds of competence practitioners sometimes display in unique, uncertain, and conflicted situations of practice. Note, however, that their artistry is a high-powered, esoteric variant of the more familiar sorts of competence all of us exhibit every day in countless acts of recognition, judgment, and skillful performance. What is striking about both kinds of competence is that they do not depend on our being able to describe what we know how to do or even to entertain in conscious thought the knowledge our actions reveal. As Gilbert Ryle observed, "What distinguishes sensible from silly operation is not their parentage but their procedure, and this holds no less for intellectual than for practical performances. "Intelligent" cannot be defined in terms of "intellectual" or "knowing *how*" in terms of "knowing *that*"; "thinking what I am doing" does not connote "both thinking what to do and doing it." When I do something intelligently...I am doing one thing and not two. My performance has a special procedure or manner, not special antecedents" (1949, p. 32). For similar reasons, my late friend Raymond M. Hainer spoke of 'knowing more than we can say', and Michael Polanyi, in *The Tacit Dimension* (1967), coined the term *tacit knowledge*.

Polanyi wrote, for example, about the remarkable virtuosity with which we recognise the faces of people we know. He pointed out that, when we notice a familiar face in a crowd, our experience of recognition is immediate. We are usually aware of no antecedent reasoning, no comparison of *this* face with images of other faces held in memory. We simply see the face of the person we know. And if someone should ask us how we do it, distinguishing one particular face from hundreds of others more or less similar to it, we are likely to discover that we cannot say. Usually we cannot construct a list of features particular to *this* face and distinct from the other faces around it; and even if we could do so, the immediacy of our recognition suggests that it does not proceed by a listing of features.

Polanyi has also described our ordinary tactile appreciation of the surfaces of materials, If we are asked what we feel when we explore the surface of a table with our hand, for example, we are apt to say that the table feels rough, smooth, cool, sticky, or slippery; but we are unlikely to say that we feel a certain compression or abrasion of our fingertips. Nevertheless, it must be from this kind of feeling that we get to our appreciation of the qualities of the table's surface. In Polanyi's words, we perceive *from* fingertip sensations to the qualities of the surface. Similarly, when we use a stick to probe, say, a hole in a stone wall, we focus, not on the impressions of the stick on the fingers and palm of our hand, but on the qualities of the hole – its size and shape, the surfaces of the stones around it – which we apprehend through these tacit impressions. To become skillful in the use of a tool is to learn to appreciate, directly and without intermediate reasoning, the qualities of the materials that we apprehend *through* the tacit sensations of the tool in our hand.

Often such processes of recognition or appreciation take the form of normative judgments. In the very act by which we recognise something, we also perceive it as 'right' or 'wrong'. Chris Alexander (1968) has described how craftsmen recognise the mismatch of an element to an overall pattern – his most famous example is the making of Slovakian peasant shawls – without the slightest ability or need to describe in words the norms they see as violated. And Geoffrey Vickers (1978), commenting on Alexander's example, has gone on to observe that, not only in artistic judgment but in all our ordinary judgments of the qualities of things, we can recognise and describe deviations from a norm very much more clearly than we can describe the norm itself.

This capacity seems to have a great deal to do with the way we learn new skills. A tennis teacher of my acquaintance writes, for example, that he always begins by trying to help his students get the feeling of 'hitting the ball right.' Once they recognise this feeling, like it, and learn to distinguish it from the various feelings associated with 'hitting the ball wrong', they begin to be able to detect and correct their own errors. But they usually cannot, and need not, describe what the feeling is like or by what means they produce it.

Skilled physicians speak of being able to recognise a particular disease, on occasion, the moment a person afflicted with it walks into their office. The recognition comes immediately and as a whole, and although the physician may later discover in his examination of the patient a full set of reasosn for his diagnosis, he is often unable to say just what clues triggered his immediate judgment.

Chester Barnard wrote, in the appendix to *The Functions of the Executive* (1983/1968), about our 'non-logical processes', by which he meant the skillful judgments, decisions, and actions we undertake spontaneously, without being able to state the rules or procedures we follow. A boy who has learned to throw a ball, for example, makes immediate judgments of distance and coordinates them with the bodily movements involved in the act of throwing, although he cannot say how he does so or perhaps even name the distance he estimates. A high school girl who has learned to solve quadratic equations can spontaneously perform a series of operations without being able to give an accurate description of the procedures she follows when she does so. A practiced accountant of Barnard's acquaintance could 'take a balance sheet of considerable complexity and within minutes or even seconds get a significant set of facts from it' (p. 306), although he could not describe in words the judgments and calculations that entered into his performance.

In similar fashion, we learn to execute such complex performances as crawling, walking, juggling, or riding a bicycle without being able to give a verbal description evern roughly adequate to our actual performance. Indeed, if we are asked to say how we do such things, we tend to give wrong answers which, if we were to act according to them, would get us into trouble. When people who know how to ride a bicycle are asked, for example, how to keep from falling when the bicycle begins to tilt to their left, some of them say that they regain their balance by turning the wheel to their right. If they actually did so, they would be likely to fall; fortunately, however, the know-how implicit in their actions is incongruent with their description of it.

I shall use *knowing-in-action* to refer to the sorts of know-how we reveal in our intelligent action—publicly observable, physical performances like riding a bicycle and private operations like instant analysis of a balance sheet. In both cases, the knowing is in the action. We reveal it by our spontaneous, skillful execution of the performance; and we are characteristically unable to make it verbally explicit.

Nevertheless, it is sometimes possible, by observing and reflecting on our actions, to make a description of the tacit knowing implicit in them. Our descriptions are of different kinds, depending on our purposes and the languages of description available to us. We may refer, for example, to the sequences of operations and procedures we execute; the clues we observe and the rules we follow; or the values, strategies, and assumptions that make up our 'theories' of action.

Whatever language we may employ, however, our descriptions of knowing-in-action are always *constructions*. They are always attempts to put into explicit, symbolic form a kind of intelligence that begins by being tacit and spontaneous. Our descriptions are conjectures that need to be tested against observation of their originals—which, in at least one respect, they are bound to distort. For knowing-in-action is dynamic, and 'facts', "procedures', 'rules', and 'theorites' are static. When we know how to catch a ball, for example, we anticipate the ball's coming by the way we extend and cup our hands and by the on-line adjustments we make as the ball approaches. Catching a ball is a continuous activity in which awareness, appreciation, and adjustment play their parts. Similarly, sawing along a penciled line requires a more or less continuous process of detecting and correcting deviations from the line. Indeed, it is this on-line anticipation and adjustments, this continuous detection and correction of error, that leads us, in the first place, to call activity 'intelligent'. Knowing suggests the dynamic quality of knowing-in-action, which, when we describe it, we convert to knowledge-in-action.

Reflection-in-Action

When we have learned how to do something, we can execute smooth sequences of activity, recognition, decision, and adjustment without having, as we say, to 'think about it.' Our spontaneous knowing-in-action usually gets us through the day. On occasion, however, it doesn't. A familiar routine produces an unexpected result; an error stubbornly resists correction; or, although the usual actions produce the usual outcomes, we find something odd about them because, for some reason, we have begun to look at them in a new way. All such experiences, pleasant and unpleasant, contain an element of *surprise.* Something fails to meet our expectations. In an attempt to preserve the constancy of our usual patterns of knowing-in-action, we may respond to surprise by brushing it aside, selectively inattending to the signals that produce it. Or we may respond to it by reflection, and we may do so in one of two ways.

We may reflect *on* action, thinking back on what we have done in order to discover how our knowing-in-action may have contributed to an unexpected outcome. We may do so after the fact, in tranquility, or we may pause in the midst of action to make what Hannah Arendt (1971) calls a 'stop-and-think.' In either case, our reflection has no direct connection to present action. Alternatively, we may reflect in the midst of action without interrupting it. In an *action-present* – a period of time, variable with the context, during which we can still make a difference to the situation at hand – our thinking serves to reshape what we are doing while we are doing it. I shall say, in cases like this, that we reflect-in-action.

Recently, for example, I built a gate out of wooden pickets and strapping. I had made a drawing and figured out the dimensions I wanted, but I had not reckoned with the problem of keeping the structure square. As I began to nail the strapping to the pickets, I noticed a wobble. I knew the structure would become rigid when I nailed in a diagonal piece, but how could I be sure it would be square? There came to mind a vague memory about diagonals: in a rectangle diagonals are equal. I took a yardstick, intending to measure the diagonals, but I found I could not use it without disturbing the structure. It occurred to me to use a piece of string. Then it became apparent that, in order to measure the diagonals, I needed a precise location at each corner. After several trials, I found I could locate the center point at each corner by constructing diagonals there (see illustration). I hammered in a nail at each of the four center points and used the nails as anchors for the measurement string. It took several minutes to figure out how to adjust the structure so as to correct the errors I found by measuring. And then, when I had the diagonals equal, I nailed in a piece of strapping to freeze the structure.

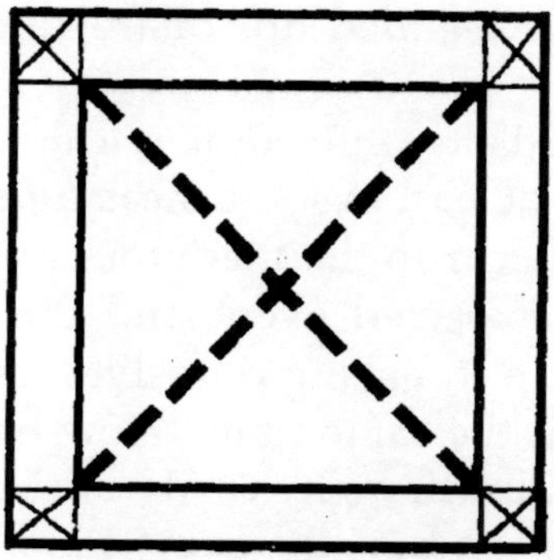

Here, in an example that must have its analogues in the experiences of amateur carpenters the world over, my intuitive way of going about the task led me to a surprise (the discovery of the wobble), which I interpreted as a problem. In the midst of action, I invented procedures to solve the problem, discovered further unpleasant surprises, and made further corrective inventions, including the several minor ones necessary to carry out the idea of using string to measure the diagonals. We might call such a process 'trial and error.' But the trials are not randomly related to one another; reflection on each trial and its results sets the stage for the next trial. Such a pattern of inquiry is better described as a sequence of 'moments' in a process of reflection-in-action:

- There is, to begin with, a situation of action to which we bring spontaneous, routinised responses. These reveal knowing-in-action that may be described in terms of strategies, understandings of phenomena, and ways of framing a task or problem appropriate to the situation. The knowing-in-action is tacit, spontaneously delivered without conscious deliberation; and it works, yielding intended outcomes so long as the situation falls within the boundaries of what we have learned to treat as normal.

- Routine responses produce a surprise—an unexpected outcome, pleasant or unpleasant, that does not fit the categories of our knowing-in-action. Inherent in a surprise is the fact that it gets our attention. For example, I might not have been surprised by the wobble in my gate because I might not have attended to it; the structure might not have ended up square, and I might not have noticed.
- Surprise leads to reflection within an action-present. Reflection is at least in some measure conscious, although it need not occur in the medium of words. We consider both the unexpected event and the knowing-in-action that led up to it, asking ourselves, as it were, 'What is this?' and, at the same time, 'How have I been thinking about it?' Our thought turns back on the surprising phenomenon and, at the same time, back on itself.
- Reflection-in-action has a critical functions, questioning the assumptional structure of knowing-in-action. We think critically about the thinking that got us into this fix or this opportunity; and we may, in the process, restructure strategies of action, understandings of phenomena, or ways of framing problems. In my example, the surprise triggered by my observation of the wobble led me to frame a new problem: 'How to keep the gate square?'
- Reflection gives rise to on-the-spot experiment. We think up and try out new actions intended to explore the newly observed phenomena, test our tentative understandings of them, or affirm the moves we have invented to change things for the better. With my measuring-string experiment, I tested both my understanding of squareness as equality of diagonals and the effectiveness of the procedures I had invented for determining when diagonals are equal. On-the-spot experiment may work, again in the sense of yielding intended results, or it may produce surprises that call for further reflection and experiment.

The description I have given is, of course, an idealised one. The moments of reflection-in-action are rarely as distinct from one another as I have made them out to be. The experience of surprise may present itself in such a way as to seem already interpreted. The criticism and restructuring of knowing-in-action may be compressed into a single process. But regardless of the distinctness of its moments or the constancy of their sequence, what distinguishes reflection-in-action, from other kinds of reflection is its immediate significance for action. In reflection-in-action, the rethinking of some part of our knowing-in-action leads to on-the-spot experiment and further thinking that affects what we do – in the situation at hand and perhaps also in others we shall see as similar to it.

The distinction between reflection-and knowing-in-action may be subtle. A skilled performer adjusts his responses to variations in phenomena. In his moment-by moment appreciations of a process, he deploys a wide-ranging repertoire of images of contexts and actions. So a baseball pitcher adapts his pitching style to the peculiarities of a particular batter or situation in a game. In order to counter an opponent's changing strategies, a tennis player executes split-second variations in play. We can say, in cases like these, that the performer responds to *variation* rather than *surprise* because the changes in context and response never cross the boundaries of the familiar.

However, in a kind of process that may look from the outside like the ones described above, a skilled performer can integrate reflection-in-action into the smooth performance of an ongoing task. I recently heard the story of a cellist who had been called to join in performing a new piece of chamber music. Because of illness, he missed the first few rehearsals and finally put in an appearance the day before the performance was to take place. He sat down with the other musicians and sight-read his way through the difficult part, playing it so well that the conductor had no need to reschedule the performance. As the cellist sight-read the score, he could not have known for certain where the piece was heading. Yet he must have sensed at each moment the direction of its development, picking up in his own performance the lines of development already laid down by others. He must have encountered surprises in response to which he formed, on-line, an interpretation guided by his emerging sense of the whole. And the execution of this feat left him with a newly developed understanding of the piece and how to play it that he would reveal as knowing-in-action on the day of the performance.

When good jazz musicians improvise together, they similarly display reflection-in-action smoothly integrated into ongoing performance. Listening to one another, listening to themselves, they 'feel' where the music is going and adjust their playing accordingly. A figure announced by one performer will be taken up by another, elaborated, turned into a new melody. Each player makes on-line inventions and responds to surprises triggered by the inventions of the other players. But the collective process of musical invention is organised around an underlying structure. There is a common schema of meter, melody, and harmonic development that gives the piece a predictable order. In addition, each player has at the ready a repertoire of musical figures around which he can weave variations as the opportunity arises. Improvisation consists in varying, combining, and recombining a set of figures within a schema that gives coherence to the whole piece. As the musicians feel the directions in which the music is developing, they make new sense of it. They reflect-in-action on the music they are collectively making—though not, of course, in the medium of words.

Their process resembles the familiar patterns of everyday conversation. In a good conversation—in some respects predictable and in others not-participants pick up and develop themes of talk, each spinning out variations on her repertoire of things to say. Conversation is collective verbal improvisation. At times it falls into conventional routines—the anecdote with side comments and reactions, for example, or the debate—which develop according to a pace and rhythm of interaction that the participants seem, without conscious deliberation, to work out in common within the framework of an evolving division of labour. At other times, there may be surprises, unexpected turns of phrase or directions of development to which participants invent on-the-spot responses.

In such examples, the participants are *making* something. Out of musical materials or themes of talk, they make a piece of music or a conversation, an artifact with its own meaning and coherence. Their reflection-in-action is a reflective conversation with the materials of a situation—'conversation', now, in a metaphorical sense. Each person carries out his own evolving role in the collective performance, 'listens' to the surprises—or, as I shall say, 'back talk'—that result from earlier moves, and responds through on-line production of new moves that give new meanings and directions to the development of the artifact. The process is reminiscent of Edmund Carpenter's description of the Eskimo sculptor patiently carving a reindeer bone, examining the gradually emerging shape, and finally exclaiming, 'Ah, seal!'

Like knowing-in-action, reflection-in-action is process we can deliver without being able to say what we are doing. Skillful improvisers often become tongue-tied or give obviously inadequate accounts when asked to say what they do. Clearly, it is one thing to be able to reflect-in-action and quite another to be able to reflect on our reflection-in-action so as to produce a good verbal description of it; and it is still another thing to be able to reflect on the resulting description.

But our reflection on our past reflection-in-action may indirectly shape our future action. The reflections of a Monday morning quarterback may be full of significance if the person reflecting is the quarterback who will play—and play differently because of his Monday morning quarterbacking—in next Saturday's game. As I think back on my experience with the wooden gate, I may consolidate my understanding of the problem or invent a better or more general solution to it. If I do, my present refection on my earlier reflection-in-action begins a dialogue of thinking and doing through which I become a more skillful (though still amateur) carpenter. Indeed these several levels and kinds of reflection play important roles in the acquisition of artistry.

Practice

So far in this article, I have shifted focus from the specialised and esoteric artistry of professional practice to the more mundane—but no less remarkable—artistry of everyday life. I have done so in order to show that knowing-in-action and reflection-in-action enter into experiences of thinking and doing that everyone shares; when we learn the artistry of a professional practice—no matter how disjunct from ordinary life it may at first appear to be—we learn new ways of using *kinds* of competences we already possess.

Nevertheless, the context of a professional practice is significantly different from other contexts; and the roles of knowing—and reflection-in-action in professional artistry, correspondingly different.

Everett Hughes defined a professional as one who makes a claim to extraordinary knowledge in matters of great human importance (Hughes, 1959). He saw the professional's claim to extraordinary knowledge as bound up in a paradigmatic bargain with society. In return for access to his special knowledge, the professional is accorded a special mandate for social control in matters of his expertise, a license to determine who shall enter his profession, and a relatively high degree of autonomy in the regulation of his practice. Thus, in close association with the very idea of a profession, we find the idea of a community of practitioners whose special knowledge sets them off from other individuals in relation to whom they hold special rights and privileges.

A professional practice is the province of a community of practitioners who share, in John Dewey's term, the traditions of a calling. They share conventions of action that include distinctive media, languages, and tools. They operate within particular kinds of institutional settings—the law court, the school, the hospital, and the business firm, for example. Their practices are structured in terms of particular kinds of units of activity—cases, patient visits, or lessons, for example—and they are socially and institutionally patterned so as to present repetitive occurrences of particular kinds of situations. A 'practice' is made up of chunks of activity, divisible into more or less familiar types, each of which is seen as calling for the exercise of a certain kind of knowledge.

Practitioners of a profession differ from one another, of course, in their subspecialties, the particular experiences and perspectives they bring to their works, and their styles of operation. But they also share a common body of explicit, more or less systematically organised professional knowledge and what Geoffrey Vickers has called an 'appreciative system'—the set of values, preferences, and norms in terms of which they make sense of practice situations, formulate goals and directions for action, and determine what constitutes acceptable professional conduct.

A professional's knowing-in-action is embedded in the socially and institutionally structured context shared by a community of practitioners. Knowing-in-*practice* is exercised in the institutional settings particular to the profession, organised in terms of its characteristic units of activity and its familiar types of practice situations, and constrained or facilitated by its common body of professional knowledge and its appreciative system.

So much we can say without making explicit reference to a particular epistemology of professional practice. Beyond this point, however, our view of a practitioner's knowing will greatly affect our descriptions of the functions and interactions of professional knowledge and professional artistry.

From the perspective of *technical rationality*, a competent practitioner is always concerned with instrumental problems. She searches for the means best suited to the achievement of fixed, unambiguous ends—in medicine, health; in law, success at litigation; in business, profit—and her effectiveness is measured by her success in finding, in each instance, the actions that produce the intended effects consistent with her objectives. In this view, *professional* competence consists in the application of theories and techniques derived from systematic, preferably scientific research to the solution of the instrumental problems of the practice.

From this perspective, we can distinguish two kinds of practice situations and two kinds of knowing appropriate to them.

There are familiar situations where the practitioner can solve the problem by routine application of facts, rules, and procedures derived from the body of professional knowledge. In city planning, for example, there are rules of thumb by which a planner can calculate, under a given zoning bylaw, the number of parking spaces required for each living unit in an apartment building. In medicine, there are routine diagnostic work-ups of patients and routine prescriptions for familiar, uncomplicated complaints.

There are also unfamiliar situations where the problem is not initially clear and there is no obvious fit between the characteristics of the situation and the available body of theories and techniques. It is common, in these types of situations, to speak of 'thinking like a doctor'—or lawyer or manager—to refer to the kinds of inquiry by which competent practitioners bring available knowledge to bear on practice situations where its application is problematic. In this sense, the familiar law school drill takes students through a process that begins with a statement of 'the facts of the case' and proceeds through characteristic patterns of reasoning to determine what legal questions are centrally at stake in the case and what judicial precedents are most pertinent to it. Similarly, medical students learn to 'take a present illness' where, starting from standardised observations, physical examinations, interviews, and laboratory tests, the student must reason his way to a plausible diagnosis of the patient's illness and a proposed strategy of treatment.

From the perspective of technical rationality, 'thinking like a—' must be thought to consist in rule-governed inquiry. The competent practitioner is seen as following rules for data gathering, inference, and hypothesis testing, which allow him to make clear connections between presenting situations and the body of professional knowledge, where such connections are initially problematic. Such rules are presumed to be explicable, where they are not already explicit. The currently popular 'expert systems', in clinical medicine as in other fields, are attempts to make explicit the information bases, rules, and procedures by which professional knowledge is applied to particular problematic cases (Kassirer and Gorry, 1970).

Within this framework, there is little room for professional artistry, except as a matter of style grafted onto technical expertise. One might recognise the existence of professional artists capable of making sense of unique or uncertain situations, but there is no way to talk sensibly about their artistry—except, perhaps, to say that they are following rules that have not yet been made explicit.

On the alternative epistemology of practice suggested here, professional artistry is understood in terms of reflection-in-action, and it plays a central role in the description of professional competence.

On this view, we would recognise as a limiting case the situations in which it is possible to make a routine application of existing rules and procedures to the fact of particular problematic situations. Beyond these situations, familiar rules, theories, and techniques are put to work in concrete instances through the intermediary of an art that consists in a limited form of reflection-in-action. And beyond these, we would recognise cases of problematic diagnosis in which practitioners not only follow rules of inquiry but also sometimes respond to surprising findings by inventing new rules, on the spot. This kind of reflection-in-action is central to the artistry with which practitioners sometimes make new sense of uncertain, unique, or conflicted situations. For example:

- A physician, aware that about 85 percent of the cases that come into her office are not 'in the book', responds to a patient's unique array of symptoms by inventing and testing a new diagnosis.
- A market researcher, monitoring consumer's reactions to a new product, discovers that they have seen in the product uses he never intended and responds by rethinking the product in terms of the consumer's discoveries.

In such cases, the practitioner experiences a surprise that leads her to rethink her knowing-in-action in ways that go beyond available rules, facts, theories, and operations. She responds to the unexpected or anomalous by restructuring some of her strategies of action, theories of phenomena, or ways of framing the problem; and she invents on-the-spot experiments to put her new understandings tot he test. She behaves more like a researcher trying to model an expert system than like the 'expert' whose behaviour is modeled.

Underlying this view of the practitioner's reflection-in-action is a *constructionist* view of the reality with which the practitioner deals—a view that leads us to see the practitioner as constructing situations of his practice, not only in the exercise of professional artistry but also in all other modes of professional competence.

Technical rationality rests on an *objectivist* view of the relation of the knowing practitioner to the reality he knows. On this view, facts are what they are, and the truth of beliefs is strictly testable by reference to them. All meaningful disagreements are resolvable, at least in principle, by reference to the facts. And professional knowledge rests on a foundation of facts.

In the constructionist view, our perceptions, appreciations, and beliefs are rooted in worlds of our own making that we come to *accept* as reality. Communities of practitioners are continually engaged in what Nelson Goodman (1978) calls 'worldmaking'. Through countless acts of attention and inattention, naming, sensemaking, boundary setting, and control, they make and maintain the worlds matched to their professional knowledge and know-how. They are in transaction with their practice worlds, framing the problems that arise in practice situations and shaping the situations to fit the frames, framing their roles and constructing practice situations to make their role-frames operational. They have, in short, a particular, professional way of seeing their world and a way of constructing and maintaining the world as they see it. When practitioners respond to the indeterminate zones of practice by holding a reflective conversation with the materials of their situations, they remake a part of their practice world and thereby reveal the usually tacit processes of worldmaking that underlie all of their practice.

Practicum

When someone learns a practice, he is initiated into the traditions of a community of practitioners and the practice world they inhabit. He learns their conventions, constraints, languages, and appreciative systems, their repertoire of exemplars, systematic knowledge, and patterns of knowing-in-action.

He may do so in one of several ways. Rarely, he may learn the practice on his own, as people sometimes learn hunting, carpentry, or the criminal trades. He may become an apprentice to senior practitioners, as many craftsmen, industrial workers, and professionals still do. Or he may enter a practicum.

Picking up a practice on one's own has the advantage of freedom—freedom to experiment without the constraints of received views. But it also has the disadvantage of requiring each student to reinvent the wheel, gaining little or nothing from the accumulated experience of others. Apprenticeship offers direct exposure to real conditions of practice and patterns of work. But most offices, factories, firms, and clinics are not set up for the demanding tasks of initiation and education. Pressures for performance tend to be high; time, at a premium; and mistakes, costly. Senior professionals have learned, in addition, to expect apprentices to come equipped with rudimentary practice skills. Nevertheless, many novices still learn through apprenticeship, and many senior practitioners and critics of professional education still see it as the method of choice.

A practicum is a setting designed for the task of learning a practice. In a context that approximates a practice world, students learn by doing, although their doing usually falls short of real-world work. They learn by undertaking projects that simulate and simplify practice; or they take on real-world projects under close supervision. The practicum is a virtual world, relatively free of the pressures, distractions, and risks of the real one, to which, nevertheless, it refers. It stands in an intermediate space between the practice world, the 'lay' world of ordinary life, and the esoteric world of the academy. It is also a collective world in its own right, with its own mix of materials tools, languages, and appreciations. It embodies particular ways of seing, thinking, and doing that tend, over time, as far as the student is concerned, to assert themselves with increasing authority.

When a student enters a practicum, she is presented, explicitly or implicitly, with certain fundamental tasks. She must learn to recognise competent practice. She must build an image of it, an appreciation of where she stands in relation to it, and a map of the path by which she can get from where she is to where she wants to be. She must come to terms with the claims implicit in the practicum: that a practice exists, worth learning, learnable by her, and represented in its essential features by the practicum. She must learn the 'practice of the practicum'—its tools, methods, projects, and possibilities—and assimilate to it her emerging image of how she can best learn what she wants to learn.

The work of the practicum is accomplished through some combination of the student's learning by doing, her interactions with coaches and fellow students and a more diffuse process of 'background learning.'

Students practice in a double sense. In simulated, partial, or protected form, they engage in the practice they wish to learn. But they also practice; as one practices the piano, the analogues in their fields of the pianist's scales and arpeggios. They do these things under the guidance of a senior practitioner, a studio master, supervising physician, or case instructor, for example. From time to time, these individuals may teach in the conventional sense, communicating information, advocating theories, describing examples of practice. Mainly, however, they function as coaches whose main activities are demonstrating, advising, questioning, and criticising.

Most practicums involve groups of students who are often as important to one another as the coach. Sometimes they play the coach's role. And it is through the medium of the group that a student can immerse himself in the world of the practicum – the all-encompassing worlds of a design studio, a musical conservatory, or psychoanalytic supervision, for example – learning new habits of thought and action. Learning by exposure and immersion, *background* learning, often proceeds without conscious awareness, although a student may become aware of it later on, as he moves into a different setting.

Our view of the work of the practicum and the conditions and processes appropriate to it depends in part on our view of the kinds of knowing essential to professional competence. The types of knowing described in the previous section, and the different perspectives on them set forth there, suggest different conceptions of a practicum.

If we see professional knowledge in terms of facts, rules, and procedures applied nonproblematically to instrumental problems, we will see the practicum in its entirety as a form of technical training. It will be the business of the instructor to communicate and demonstrate the application of rules and operations to the facts of practice. One might imagine, on this view, a practicum for learning a computer language, techniques of analytic chemistry, or methods of statistical analysis. Students would be expected to acquire the material by reading, listening and watching, familiarising themselves with examples of practice problems matched to the appropriate categories of theory and technique. Coaching would consist in observing student performance, detecting errors of application, pointing our correct responses.

If we see professional knowing in terms of 'thinking like a' manager, lawyer, or teacher, students will still learn relevant facts and operations but will also learn the forms of inquiry by which competent practitioners reason their way, in problematic instances, to clear connections between general knowledge and particular cases. The standard drills of the law school classroom and the medical clinic exemplify this view. In a practicum of this kind, there is presumed to be a right answer for every situation, some item in the corpus of professional knowledge that can be seen, eventually, to fit the case at hand. But, depending on one's view of 'thinking like a—', coaches may emphasize either the *rules* of inquiry or the reflection-in-action by which, on occasion, students must develop new rules and methods of their own.

If we focus on the kinds of reflection-in-action through which practitioners sometimes make new sense of uncertain, unique or conflicted situations of practice, then we will assume neither that existing professional knowledge fits every case nor that every problem has a right answer. We will see students as having to learn a kind of reflection-in-action that goes beyond statable rules—not only by devising new methods of reasoning, as above, but also by constructing and testing new categories of understanding, strategies of action, and ways of framing problems. Coaches will emphasize indeterminate zones of practice and reflective conversations with the materials of a situation.

It is important to add that the third kind of practicum need not obviate the work of the first and second. Perhaps we lear to reflect-in-action by learning first to recognise and apply standard rules, facts, and operations; then to reason from general rules to problematic cases, in ways characteristic of the profession; and only then to develop and test new forms of understanding and action where familiar categories and ways of thinking fail.*

---

* There are two points here, and they are of equal importance. The first is that the knowing-in-action characteristic of competent practitioners in a professional field is not the same as the professional knowledge taught in the schools; in any given case, the relationship of the two kinds of knowledge should be treated as an open question. Ordinary knowiing-in-action may be an application of research-based professional knowledge taught in the schools, may be overlapping with it, or may have nothing to do with it. This point is similar to the one made by Charles Lindblom and David Cohen in *Usable Knowledge* (1979).

The second point is that competent professional practitioners often have the capacity to generate new knowing-in-action through reflection-in-action undertaken in the indeterminate zones of practice. The sources of knowing-in-action include this reflection-in-action and are not limited to research produced by university-based professional schools.

Practicums of the third kind exist, in greater or lesser degree, in the deviant traditions of studio and conservatory. They are sometimes also found in association with apprenticeships or—less often, and usually without formal legitimacy or status—in the clinics, workshops, and internships of professional schools. These practicums are reflective in that they aim at helping students learn to become proficient at a kind of reflection-in-action. They are reflective in the further sense that they depend for their effectiveness on a reciprocally reflective dialogue of coach and student.

Index

Accounting for Accounting 93-98
Accounting and Public Policy 84-86
Accounting and that Which Happens in Its Name 98-99
Alken and Hague 20
Allaire and Firsirotu 121, 127
Allen and Kraft 119
Allison and Halperin 100, 103
American Council of Deans 53
Arendt, H. 190
Arnold 101
Arnold and Feldman 80
AT ZT 81-82, 174, 180
Aubert 109

Bachrach and Baratz 22
Bahruveller 84
Bahrami and Evans 70
Bailyn 68-72, 78, 751
Bailyn and Lynch 71
Baker 119
Bardach 100
Barnard, Chester 188
Bell telephone System 64
Bourgeois and Eisenstadt 70, 150
Brown University 31
Bureaucrclies as Instrument of Policy 101-05
Business Week 121, 177, 183

Churchill 40, 45, 50
Cohen 126, 129
Coordination : Its means and Political Relevance 2-7
Components and Dimensions 7-9
Cronbach *et al.* 107
Crozier 104

Deal and Kennedy 124
De Pree, Max 56-63
Derthick 104
Donne, J. 64
Dowd and Sonnenfild 80
Downs 104
Drucker, Peter F. 24-30, 56-63, 68-69
Durkheim 112

Edward VII 49
Edwards and Sharkarsky 100
Elmore 103
Elster 107
Emerson 21

Feldman 80, 82
Finkelskin and Newmen 150
Fortune Magazine 121

Galbraith 122-23
Geertz 126-27

General Motors 64
Giddens 120
Glennerster 1
Gluckman 131
Good year 75
Gregory 120-21, 125

Hall 80
Hallenberg 73
Hanf and Schanpf 100, 103
Hannan and Free 71
Harris and Cronen 124
Hawkes 137
Hayek 13
Healey 73
Hesselbein 24-30
Hewlett-Packard 80, 174
Hirschleifer and Riley 104
Hitler 124
Houser, Ted
Hughes 69, 196

IBM 52, 75, 174
Information : Coping with Overload 14-16

Jacobsen 106
JASP 1
Jennings, Peter 138

Kant 142
Kanter 119
Kaplan 97
Kassirer and Gorry 198
Keesing 28, 117
Kellogg Graduate School of Management 143
Kerr 73, 77
Kerr and Slocum 174
Kilmann 117, 174
Kilmann *et al.* 117
Kleingartner and Anderson 152, 159

Kornhouser 73
Kuper 117

Lazarsfeld 83
Levine 100
Lindblom 19
Lochen and Martinsen 106
Lowi 106
Lukes 21
Lynch 68
Lynn 103

MacArthur, Douglas 52
Malinowski 120
Management of Human Resources 152-54
March 106-07
March and Olsen 101, 104, 111
Marshall 100
Martin *et al.* 130
March and Simon 104
Mayhew 100
Meek 130
Metzer and Von Glinnou 79
Meyer 96
Meyer and Rowan 96
Miller 68, 71, 73, 75, 79-80, 82
Morgarn 124
Morgar, Hall, and Martier 80-81

Napoleon 34
National Coal Board 84
Newyork Times 139, 142
New York University 4,

Olofson and Sualander 86
On Examining the Practices of Accounting 90-93
OH 115-16
Ouchi 121
Oyen 110

Page 109

Peters and Waterman 124, 174
Pettigrew 126, 131
Polanyi 186-88
Policy : A Misleading Concept 16-18
Policy-Making and Policy Ambiguity 107-111
Polanyi 186-88
Popper 13
Power Dependence and Organisational Interactions 18-23
Pressman and Wildavsky 1, 100, 104
Pressures for Public Sector Accounting to change 86-90
Programs for Reforms of the Policy Process 105-07

Raclin 73, 75
Raiffer 107
Riggs 75
Robbe-Grillet 137
Roebuck 64
Roosevelt, Franklin 49-50, 107

Sabatier and Mazmaniar 106
Sacco and Knopka 75
Sactren 109
Schein 119, 174
Schoonhoven and Eisenstadt 69-70
Schriesheim, Von Glinow and kerr 73, 77-78
Schwartz and Davis 117, 124
Sears 64
Secrist 73
Sethia and Von Glinow 173-77, 183
Shakespeare 49, 134
Simmonds 97
Smircich 121, 124
Snow, C.P. 121
Sophocles 134-36
St. Augustine 40
Stinchcombe 70
Stinger 126, 132
Stonich 175
Sutherland 102

Turner 45-16, 123

Vickers, Geoffrey 187, 196
Von Glinow 179-80
Von Glinow, Driver, Brouffear and Prince 82

Wall Street Journal 139
Walker and Gutteridge 79
Watson, Tom 52
Weber, Max 126
Weick 111, 124
Westinghouse 75
World War I 49
World War II 64, 137